BRAND

THE DRAMA LIBRARY

General Editor: EDWARD THOMPSON

HENRIK IBSEN

BRAND

A NEW STAGE VERSION BY
JAMES FORSYTH

WITH AN INTRODUCTION BY
TYRONE GUTHRIE

HEINEMANN
LONDON MELBOURNE TORONTO

William Heinemann Ltd
LONDON MELBOURNE TORONTO
CAPE TOWN AUCKLAND
THE HAGUE

© 1960, James Forsyth

First published 1960

PUBLISHED BY
WILLIAM HEINEMANN LTD
15-16 QUEEN STREET, LONDON, WCI
PRINTED IN GREAT BRITAIN BY THE
WINDMILL PRESS LTD KINGSWOOD, SURREY

FOREWORD

In preparing a new version of *Brand* it seemed to me that a new approach was needed and that it had to be one which would face these facts:

That it is only possible to convert the original of such a work into another language and still retain its vitality if there is in the process some element of re-creation.

That, in order to make the great length of the original conform to the practical needs of the English stage now, some process of condensing rather than cutting is required. Mere cutting at such a complex structure would probably result in the destruction of vital parts, and the distortion of the total shape of the original.

And that, as *Brand* is a work of poetic vision the writer of any stage version must be committed to some form of dramatic poetry as the basis of speech. Further, in the interests of both vitality and truth, this should be a poetry which is not just imitative of the original. It should not, as it were, be running parallel to it and therefore at a remove from its subject matter, but be some form natural to the writer by which he can get to grips with the subject matter. It seemed a fortunate thing that Ibsen used a free-ranging four foot line and that a four stress rhythm is a natural one for me.

This version is intended to be a work of re-creation, not with the immodest hope of improving on the original (except in the matter of shaping it to the stage at the moment) but in the belief that there is no other way possible to prepare this great work for the English stage.

I would not have been able to undertake this work without the vital, scholarly assistance of Evelyn Ramsden in preparing, passage by passage, literal versions of the Norwegian original; and often many alternatives of these.

All the liberties I may have taken are in the interests of the great man who was beyond consultation, but present, I hope, in spirit.

Anstye, 1960   JAMES FORSYTH.

INTRODUCTION

BY

TYRONE GUTHRIE

BRAND is possibly Ibsen's greatest play. Two main difficulties have stood between BRAND and the English-speaking public: the great length of the original and the fact that it is a work of poetic vision and has been hard material to translate into the terms of either another language or another theatre.

To surmount these difficulties demanded a poetic imagination competent to carry Ibsen's vision, and a playwright's skill competent to reduce the original to workable stage proportions. It is not so difficult to find either of these qualifications on its own, but to find both in one writer, is unusual. James Forsyth's service to Ibsen in this piece of work has been a very real one. I think that the genius of one author has combined with the inspiration of a second to give us a new work of art, which, by its very 'free-'ness, has captured more truthfully the original spirit and intention of Ibsen than has – with all due deference to Archer and others – many another more purely literary and 'faithful' version. Both the problem of language and the problem of condensing (as opposed to cutting) have been faced in such a way that the power of the play has not been diminished. On the contrary, for my part I find this condensed version more powerful as well as more manageable than the tremendously long original. However painstaking a scholarly translation may be, it can hardly hope to produce other than a work which is, as it were, a crib to the original rather than a work of art in its own right. If a work has to cross from the Norwegian to the English and retain a speech vital both to its spirit and to the practice of acting, there must be 'liberties taken'. In this case the liberties have been taken courageously and with integrity towards the aim of the original.

The measure of its success seems to me to be apparent in these things: that we have a depth of characterisation which one expects of Ibsen and which is by no means unusual in Forsyth's plays; that the vitality of the language of these characters is tied to locale, setting, argument, with a reality that is never in doubt; that, finally, the power to move the imagination at several levels of imagery which is so characteristic of Ibsen, is neither lost nor thwarted by a junior partner in the Art who has a reputation for just this sort of thing. This all seems to me to add up to a rather happy partnership. Certainly I welcome the emergence of this vital version of a work which, in its argument, its vision and the form of theatre it implies, is excitingly appropriate to the present time and to current trends in the serious theatre, whether in Britain or America.

THE CHARACTERS

BRAND a Norwegian pastor

HIS MOTHER an old woman

EINAR an artist

AGNES a young woman

THE SHERIFF the local Government Officer

THE DOCTOR a middle-aged man

THE DEAN of the diocese

THE SEXTON of the Parish Church

THE SCHOOLMASTER of the parish

GERD a mad gypsy girl

A MAN of the locality (a small-holder)

HIS SON

A GYPSY WOMAN

A FISHERMAN a spokesman of the people of the
fjord.

A CROWD of men, women and children of the
fjord and surrounding district.

THE VISIONARY FIGURE OF AGNES

A VOICE

SYNOPSIS OF SCENES

The action takes place in 1866 or thereabouts, partly in, and around a fjord village on the northern part of the west coast of Norway.

ACT ONE

SCENE 1 : (A) A part of the coastal plateau.
(B) The same – higher up.
(C) A high part of the plateau immediately above the Fjord.
Spring, early morning.

SCENE 2 : Down on a Point jutting out into the Fjord.
Late afternoon of the same day.

ACT TWO

SCENE 1 : The Garden of the Pastor's house.
Three years later.

SCENE 2 : Inside the Pastor's house.
Christmas Eve of the same year.

ACT THREE

SCENE 1 : Outside the New Church.
Some months later – a spring morning.

SCENE 2 : Same as Act 1, Scene 1 (C).
Towards evening – the same day.

ACT I

Scene I (A)

Up among the snows on a high coastal plateau. It is around dawn.

(*Note: Scene 1 is divided into three sub-scenes which occur on various parts of the same coastal plateau, as* BRAND *progresses towards his home Fjord.*)

Dimly seen, BRAND *comes in from the East. He is dressed in black and carries a staff and a wallet.*

MAN (*off – calling*): Hi! Not so fast! Hi, stranger! Where are you now?

BRAND: I'm here. (*Calling him on*) Here, man! *Here!*

    A MAN *and his* SON *follow stumbling in the half-dark.*

MAN: You'll lose yourself, stranger. (*Looking round*) By Jesu! What a mist! I could hardly see the length of my stick.

SON: Father – there are gullies over this way!

MAN: I'm afraid we've lost the path, sir.

BRAND: Then we must find it again. (*Beginning to search*).

MAN: Stop! (*Shrieking.*) Good God, man! – The surface here is only a crust of frozen snow. Don't *stamp* on it! (*As* BRAND *taps with his staff.*) Go easy, do you hear?

BRAND: Quiet! (*Listening.*) I can hear the roar of water. (*Surprised.*) It's right under my feet!

MAN: That will be a mountain torrent, sir,
carving out a great abyss
deep underneath this crust of snow.
It may be miles down; and if we got through. . . .
Stop! I tell you!

BRAND (*searching again*): I cannot. I *must go on.*

1

MAN: But all this is just a false crust.
It's death to cross it.

BRAND (*moving on step-by-step*): Yet cross it I must.
I have an urgent message to deliver.

MAN: Let it wait for the dawn.

BRAND: My particular message is from one
who will not wait for a rising sun.

MAN (*cautiously following in* BRAND's *footsteps*): If your message
were from the Lord God himself ...

BRAND (*quickly*): ... But, my friend, I believe it *is*.

MAN: What? (*Stopping*)

SON: Father, I'm frightened.
The surface under us is giving way.
It's the thaw!

MAN (*restraining* BRAND): Now listen . . . sir—— The days of
miracles are gone. There are some things which a man cannot
do—— And *this* is one of them! Crossing this bit of the hills
before dawn is utter madness. And I, for one, must think of my
wife and the child at home.

BRAND: Turn back if you must. I cannot.

MAN (*hesitating*): You think I'm afraid?

BRAND (*facing him*): I recognise Fear when I see it.

Distant rumble of avalanche

SON: The snow's on the move! (*Shouting*) That's an avalanche,
Father!

MAN: An avalanche above your head
and an abyss beneath your feet!
Does that not convince you now
that you're simply throwing your life away?

BRAND: No. (*With a smile*)
For if God asks for my life in this,
then, welcome your avalanche *and* your abyss!

(*Turning to go*) You see, I have found the path.
Good-day!

    BRAND *picks his way forward as the noise of the avalanche grows.*

MAN: He must be crazy! (*Retreating*) He's going on!

Avalanche nearer.

SON: Father! The avalanche! It's coming this way! (*In panic*)
Father! Father! Come! Come!

The SON *almost drags his* FATHER *off as the thunder of the avalanche
reaches its height and the scene and* BRAND *are swallowed up in noise
and darkness.*

SCENE I (B) *The same – higher up.*

As the thunder of the avalanche passes away the light of dawn increases.
BRAND *is revealed, as though climbing. He stops to look back in the
direction taken by the Man and his Son.*

BRAND: There they go! – like father, like son!
  – with one thought only in their minds:
to save their own skins.
Fear – Oh, that enemy——

He sits to rest.

Fear! (*Watching the rising sun*)
                    When I was a boy——
two ideas possessed me:—
an Owl who was frightened of the dark,
and a Fish who was terrified of the sea!
(*He laughs*)
I'd try to banish them both from my brain,
but each time they'd wriggle back again,
and I'd laugh – laugh uncontrollably. Why?
Because in my childish way I had seen
that paradox which in every man
makes him most fear what most he'd wish.
Because every man in sickness or health
is such an Owl and such a Fish;
and, destined to toil in this hushed sea of stars

shuttered in by infinite night,
he has one overwhelming wish –
to reach the loud shores in a blinding light!

The light of the sun breaks through. There comes the sound of several voices singing in the distance. BRAND *rises, troubled.*

Singing? Up here? ...

The singing dies away

(Shading his eyes and looking)

Only the great clean sheets of snow
laid out for Norways's mornings. No.

(Sighting something nearer)

Sound of laughter off and approaching.

BRAND: A girl and a man ... and both so happy.

As BRAND *watches from the rock, the laughter grows near and* AGNES *runs in, pursued by* EINAR.

They are both young, in glowing health, and lightly dressed for their tramp over the moors.

Breathless, AGNES *is overtaken by* EINAR, *who clasps her in his arms. They do not notice* BRAND, *who stands above them.*

EINAR *(playfully improvising)*:
Agnes, my exquisite butterfly,
Now for my magic to trap you:
I weave this intricate network or verse;
In whose mesh of rhyme I shall wrap you.

They both laugh at the patent artificiality of their game.

AGNES *(taking up the challenge)*:
Einar, if I am a butterfly,
You may from the heather bells lure me
To play for a time your game of rhyme;
But *(She breaks free)* these arms will never secure me!

Laughing, she tries to elude Einar's pursuit. Unwittingly they approach the edge of a crevasse.

BRAND: *Stop!!*

  They stop, puzzled and surprised at this cry.

EINAR: Who was that? (*Afraid*)

AGNES: Look! (*Pointing to* BRAND)

BRAND: Go back! You are on the edge of a great abyss!

EINAR: Not one that frightens me – nor her.

AGNES: Besides, we have not finished our game.
 This was to last a lifetime.

EINAR (*embracing her*): A hundred years!

BRAND: It will take rather less than that time to crash to the
 bottom of that abyss!

EINAR: Oh! (*Realising the actual danger*) It *is* a crevasse.

AGNES: We would have continued our game, sir, in Heaven.

EINAR: Come and join us. (*Laughing yet moving in from the edge*)
 Don't stand up there,
 like a black snowman.

  As BRAND *moves to come down*

I am an artist, my friend,
and *this* is AGNES – my bride-to-be.

  BRAND, *coming down, stops just above them.*

We've come from our engagement party——
at her old friend the doctor's – across the plateau.
We've just left our friends down below on the hill.

AGNES (*making conversation as* BRAND *says nothing*):
 They sang and danced as we went. It was lovely.
 We danced almost the whole way up here.

BRAND: And now where does your way lie?

EINAR: In the first place down to the Great Fjord,
 to catch the steamer to her home
 – then the wedding!

BRAND: And after that?

EINAR (*jocularly*): Set sail for Southern climes!

BRAND: And then?

EINAR: Then? (*Smiling at* AGNES) Wedded bliss!

BRAND: I see. Then I'll bid you – not happiness, but joy.

EINAR (*as* BRAND *turns to go*): Wait a moment, stranger! . . . Your face . . . (*Puzzling*)

BRAND: . . . I *am* a stranger to you – now. (*Facing* EINAR)

EINAR (*staring at him*): At home or . . . Yes! . . . at school!

BRAND: At school it was. But now *I'm* no schoolboy . . . Einar.

EINAR: It *is*! Brand! Brand, what a piece of luck!

BRAND: Yes, Einar, I recognised you. (*Smiling*) Still the gay boy?

EINAR: And still the same old Brand. Ha! Yet not so long-faced, eh? (*To* AGNES) He used to freeze us all with one look of Northern scorn.

BRAND (*jokingly*): I was homeless then and on my own, among you soft southerners.

EINAR (*laughing*): But *I* am the stranger here. This is *your* home district, isn't it?

From this point the eyes of AGNES *never leave* BRAND'S *face, as she clings to* EINAR.

BRAND: Yes. My way happens to lie through it. In fact I'll pass very near my own home.

EINAR: *Pass* it? Then you're going further on?

BRAND: Oh, *much* further.

EINAR: And you're a priest? (*Looking him up and down*) Well, well!

BRAND: A roving pastor. (*Smiling*) It suits me. It leaves me free to come and go as the spirit moves.

EINAR (*lightly*): And where's the spirit moving you now?

BRAND: Ah, that's a long story. (*Seriously*) And it might just upset you both. (*Conscious of* AGNES *listening silently and watching him*).

EINAR: It would take a lot to upset us now, wouldn't it? (*To* AGNES)

BRAND: Well, the steamer you will catch in the fjord will also carry me part of my way. We'll talk aboard.

EINAR: Excellent! Agnes, (*who seems lost in thought*) he's sailing too.

BRAND: Yes, but not, I'm afraid, to your wedding. I must attend to the funeral of a mutual friend of ours, Einar.

EINAR: Dear God, who's to be buried now?

BRAND: 'Dear God.' (*Wryly*) Well, he's dead. The least we can do, is give the old chap a decent funeral.

EINAR (*with an uncertain laugh*): Brand, old boy

AGNES (*frightened*): Come, Einar.

EINAR: Wait, (*looking again at* BRAND) Brand, are you all right ... I mean ...

BRAND (*laughing*): ... As sound as a mountain pine! No, I'm not ill.
It is our age is ill, Einar – this age
where Frivolity takes the place of Joy.

EINAR: Is that meant for us? – Frivolity?
Are we in for a sermon?

BRAND: No. I'm not sermonising now.
I'm not sure I'm speaking for my church.
I'm not sure I'm a christian. I'm simply a man –
a man who would join forces with you
in deploring the total lack of joy.
in his miserable fellow countrymen.
Be drunk with pleasure if you will,
but be so *entirely*. Drink your fill!
Drink *ALL* or *Nothing*! It's the little thrill –
it's *sipping* the cup which now denies
God his true nature. It's Compromise.

EINAR: You're not going to make us responsible now
    for God's nature! (*Laughing*)

BRAND: In a way.
    As we reflect Him. We are a clay
    we also mould. You are a painter?

EINAR: Yes.

BRAND: And what is the picture you have of your God? He is
    old isn't he?

EINAR (*hesitantly*): Well . . . not young——

BRAND: And naturally – with age – he is – er – thin on top? –
    might have a hoary wisp of a beard;
    though kind, weird enough to get children scared
    into going to bed after tea;
    wears bedroom slippers – or should – shouldn't he?

EINAR (*angrily*): Now, look here!——

BRAND: Calm, Einar! I'm not mocking you.
    But isn't the God in most men's minds
    just such a figure? And . . . (*Wickedly*) you know, as well as me,
    it needs such an image of God to save
    the faces of a Church and State
    which both have one foot in the grave?

(*Becoming serious*)

But I have a God who is older still –
yet always young. My God's a storm –
yours a sighing in the wind.
Mine is all love! – yours only kind.
The voice of yours is weak – mine strong;
not a human whine – but a heavenly song
stricken from the heights above!

(*Towering above them on the rock*)

For, my God is He whose great voice came,
and with the lightning in his tongue,

thrilled through Moses as he stood
dwarfed by all infinitude
beside the bush of flame!

(*With mounting fervour*)

He stopped the sun over Gibeon!
He did wonders which might be
performed again in our own day,
were the despairing human race
not so utterly rotted by
fantasy, fear and frivolity!

EINAR (*trying to take it lightly*):
And is the human race to be
. . . revitalised, here and now?
– by you.

BRAND (*simply*): It could be. God willing.

EINAR: The new God?

BRAND: The new will. He's not *new*.
He's as old as Adam. We go back to go on.
Evidence of the old spirit is here –
in bits of virtues, in pygmies of men.
But the bits must be compounded again,
in that new man who will one day rise,
to vindicate God in God's eyes –
his *intended* Adam!

EINAR: Well . . . maybe. (*Uncomfortably*) Agnes, come.
We are going round by the West path, nearer the sea.

BRAND: If your choice is the West path, mine is the North.
It's the steepest but it's the shortest way.
At my home fjord we may meet again.

(*Turning to go*)

Until then, Einar, and . . . Agnes . . . Goodbye!

EINAR (*flatly*): Goodbye!

AGNES is *unable to reply.*

BRAND *goes.*

AGNES *moves over to where she can watch him disappear and* EINAR *keeps by her.*

EINAR (*with forced return of spirits*): Let him go his steep way! We'll get back to our ... (*Mockingly*) ... 'frivolity'! I'll take the next verse.

AGNES: No. Not now. I feel tired.

EINAR: Well – so do I. (*Trying to shake off the effect of* BRAND'S *words*)
But we'll soon be out of the mountains. Look!

(*Pointing*)

Look! Westwards! Look at that long bar of sea.
The sun breaks its surface where the morning winds
must crease it in little wavelets. See!
Can you see that little dark thread of smoke
tailing off in a long slow wisp ... (*Crying out*) That's the boat!
– the little black spider spinning the thread!
She clears the point. (*Putting his arm round her*) Our dream ship,
                                                                    dear.

This evening, when she stands out to sea,
we shall be looking back from down there
at these cold hills – if the mist lifts.
But look how it comes down again –
like a veil over our seascape. Well – (*turning to her*)
you see what a great painter our Old God is,
to paint such a sea-scene with such skies?

AGNES: Our Old God! Yes. But tell me, did you see ...

EINAR: Yes?

AGNES (*hesitantly*): Did *you* also see –
how he *grew* as he spoke?

EINAR *looks perplexed, then begins to move away.*

EINAR: Here comes the mist. Down this way.

AGNES *follows, as the scene is lost to us.*

SCENE I (C)

Further on — at the edge of the same coastal plain — a precipitous path high above the Fjord.

BRAND, *coming down the path, pauses.*

Note: *Where he stands, a great cornice of frozen snow hangs over his head. This, or a great icicle, is a suggested feature or landmark, by which the scene can immediately be recognised when it recurs as the last scene of the play.*

BRAND: Home...

BRAND *looks down into the Fjord.*

Once again, at my feet, in shadow, I see
the map of my past laid out below ...
So near by inches and feet, yet so far
by the tortuous path from that grey shore,
past the boathouses, to the last farm,
every *inch* is familiar:
those rocks, as sheer as a prison wall;
that creek whose birch roots taste the sea;
these streams now hemmed in with alders; all
these have left their mark on me.
But everything seems smaller, more grey.

(*Looking seawards*)

And the fjord! Has it always been such
a narrow, gloomy, giant's ditch?
That's a storm blowing up. A square-rigged smack
goes scudding before it towards the black shore;
and southwards, in the shadow of the cliff, I see —
a quay, a shed, and, beyond the quay,
a farmhouse, which is painted ... *red.*
Home

(*Looking down*)

Yes, here the abyss of the past lies built
across the path by which I'd run
to arrest the setting of the sun
and begin again where Man has no guilt!

Suddenly a stone is thrown from above and rolls near him.

GERD (*off*): Whoo! Whoo!

BRAND: Hi! (*Turning*) Who's that?

GERD: Me! Gerd!

BRAND: Stop throwing these stones!

GERD, *a Gypsy girl of about fifteen years of age, runs down the path with stones in her apron. She has a wild appearance.*

GERD: I hit! I hit! He screamed out! (*She throws again*)

BRAND: Stop that, girl! Don't you know that one little stone could start an avalanche?

GERD: Oh! (*Disappointed*) There he sits see-sawing on a withered branch! Not hurt at all. Whoo! . . .

She throws again.

BRAND: Stop it, I tell you!

GERD: Here he comes! (*She runs to* BRAND) Help! Oh! (*Clinging to* BRAND) *Hide me! Help! He is digging his claws into me! Ah!* . . . .

BRAND: In God's name, what is it? Who are you girl?

GERD: Sssh! I am Gerd. Who are you?

BRAND: Gerd?

GERD: Sh! Sh! Stand still! Stand still!
He's flying away. Sssssssssssssh! (*Pause*)
Now.

She moves cautiously from him, looking around.

Did you see the great hawk?

BRAND: Hawk? No.

GERD (*disappointed*): No?

GERD *turns away and begins to mount the rocks again.*

BRAND: Where are you off to now?

GERD (*mounting*) : To church.

BRAND : But the church lies down in the fjord below.

(*Pointing*)

GERD : That one? (*She smiles mockingly*) No. No.
 That one is ugly. That one is mean.

BRAND : Mean?

GERD : Yes – too *small*, much too small.

BRAND : And where could *you* have seen a larger one?

GERD : A larger one? Ah! That's my secret. (*Climbing upwards*)
 Goodbye!

BRAND : Wait, girl! Is that the way to your larger church
 – up towards the snow peaks?

GERD : Yes.
 Come with me if you'd like to know
 a church which is made of ice and snow.

BRAND : Of ice and snow?

GERD : It is *my* ice church.
 (*Possessively*)

BRAND : The Ice Church! Ah. When I was a boy I too
 called it my Ice Church. Now I know.

GERD : Under its great white roof it is safe.
 Coming?

BRAND : No, Gerd, not that way.
 I used to tip-toe over its floor.
 It is only the ice of a great rock pool –
 yet beneath the arches of drifted snow,
 through whose white vaults the light would glow,
 I too would seem to have reached the cool
 peace of a great cathedral. Yes, I know.

GERD : It may just 'seem' a cathedral to you;
 but it *is* my church. Up there I sing.

BRAND : It's not safe for you child.
And don't you throw stones! One of them
might bring the whole mass of ice and snow
crashing down here. Why, it might go
thundering on down into the fjord,
and bury the houses the church and all!

GERD (*in her own fantasy*): If you come up here, I can show
where an avalanche thawed under a cliff,
and a herd of reindeer, frozen stiff,
now stand like statues.

BRAND : Child, do you understand!
(*Shouting*) Don't go up! There death hangs by a thread!

GERD (*pointing down the fjord*):
Don't go down! There it stinks of the dead!
Ha! ha!

As she stands, poised above BRAND.

GERD : In my church the torrent sings
the Mass, and all the whisperings,
and fingering of pages, are
the winds whistling beneath the great door,
from which the avalanche will roar,
Hallelujah! ! ! (*Crying out*)
                      Here comes the hawk again!
But if I can reach my church his wings
daren't touch me. Whoooo!
I'm safe in my Ice Church! Let me alone! ! !...

GERD *goes, shrieking up the hill.*

BRAND (*watching her go*): Poor wild soul –
a prey to her own fantasies. (*Turning*)
Yet, there are sweet songs stored
in the dulcimer with the broken board,
and dullness of itself must breed
creatures neither bad nor good.
There's no hope in the dead, dull eyes,
but in the brood of evil lies
goodness ; writhing.

As BRAND *faces into the storm wind blowing in off the sea, and declaims
into the teeth of it:*

BRAND: Man's house of prayer down there below,
or Nature's up here in the ice and snow –
which is the better? And which of these three
strays furthest from the one true way?
Gerd with her *Fantasy* up in the snow,
preferring her dangerous church of ice
to the ugly, smug little one below?
Or Einar – who in *Frivolity*
pursues a transitory bliss
to the very edge of the abyss?
Or that man with his son who, in *Fear*,
neither lives nor dies? (*Above the rising wind*)

                              Oh, these three! –

Fear – Frivolity – Fantasy –
they plague the whole world!
God, keep me free of this past lying at my feet,
and in a new land let me defeat
the dragon Despair, and these his three
faithful witches!

SCENE CURTAIN

Storm, musically or otherwise interpreted covers scene-change.

SCENE 2

Down in the Fjord. On a point jutting out into the water.

*The storm has reached its climax during the scene-change, and now begins
to ebb as the scene comes into view.*

*Note: The weather process, which covers the duration of this scene, is one
starting with storm and mist, proceeding towards calm and the return
of the sun; and finally ending with the setting of the sun.*

It is now late afternoon of the same day.

BRAND (*off, and shouting above the wind*): Now! Hold her! Lash her
to the quay! The house is up here! Do not follow me! Do you
hear? Do not come in after me.

BRAND, *clambers into view over some rocks and strides across to disappear
again behind the gable of a fisherman's hut or cottage.*

*Towering over the fisherman's hut is a cliff. Between the rocks and the cliff
a path leads off and down into the gloom of the fjord. Above the rocks, the
top of a mast and a tattered bit of sail indicate the boat by which* BRAND
has just arrived.

AGNES *appears, coming up from the boat. Her hair is so windswept and
her clothes so drenched with spray that she looks like a creature rising
from the sea. Immediately after* AGNES *comes into view another figure
appears on the path above. This is the* SHERIFF. *He carries a sack
on his back.*

SHERIFF (*calling over sound of wind and sea*): Lord Almighty! What
are you?

As AGNES *turns, he approaches. Their conversation is carried on over the
noise of the abating sea.*

SHERIFF: You look like Agnes Come Out of The Sea, –
from the old legends! Who are you?

AGNES: My name *is* Agnes. But I am a stranger here.
I have just come from the village at the head of the fjord.

SHERIFF: And what possessed you to cross the fjord now?
It's a miracle you're safe. Who's with you?
Don't tell me you sailed that cockle alone;
or I'll think you *are* Agnes Out Of The Sea.

AGNES: Brand was with me.

SHERIFF: Who?

AGNES: A priest.

SHERIFF: A parson. What does he want out here?

AGNES: When we arrived at the village a woman had come,
to say that her man was dying out here.
She needed a priest for him.

SHERIFF: And this priest crossed the fjord in that storm?
Well, times have changed! And parsons too!

AGNES: They said the dying man was mad.
He had watched one child starving to death,
till he couldn't stand it. He killed the child.
And then he turned the knife on himself.

SHERIFF: Ah! dear me!

AGNES: There is a famine back in the fjord.

SHERIFF: I know it only too well, my girl;
and I can't make the food stocks last much longer.

AGNES: Why, who are you?

SHERIFF: The Sheriff, my sweet,
Just a humble instrument of the State, setting a good example by
this – collecting scraps from farm to farm.
(*He pats his sack*) I was going back with this sackful now;
but the storm has carried the footbridge away.
My clerk has men mending it. So the parson's in there?

AGNES: Yes. (*She sits on the rocks*)

SHERIFF: But why did *you* have to come?
Were there no able-bodied men
to help him with the sail?

AGNES: They did not trust him.

SHERIFF: You mean they hadn't the courage?

AGNES: Not even his own friend.

SHERIFF: So you shamed the men, eh? Brave girl!
And a brave parson! Well!—— (*Turning to go*)

AGNES: Perhaps you could help him.
There are two other children.
He won't let me go in.

SHERIFF: Eh? No. (*Shaking his head and smiling*)
   The servant of the State doesn't interfere
   with the Church's officers, my dear.
   I'll see if they've mended the footbridge yet.
   What did you say his name was?

AGNES: Brand.

SHERIFF: Brand? Name's familiar. Well . . .

                    (*Turning to go*)

here comes our bit of afternoon sun.
You get yourself clear of this famine spot.
Yes – Just you sit there and let the sun dry your hair.
And keep out of the fjord. You don't look too strong.
(*Shouldering his sack of bread*)
Now I must get back to my Great Unfed
and dispense my more solid blessing – bread!
(*With a laugh*)

           The SHERIFF *goes, by the path.*

           AGNES *sits staring out seawards.*

      Slowly BRAND *comes in from the Fisherman's hut.*

BRAND (*in a subdued voice*):
   If Abraham had sacrificed his son
   at the Devil's prompting . . . not God's . . . What a crime!
   Those two children are stained for life
   by the sight of his hand raising the knife
   in this false sacrifice. Could he not see –
   or had he not the will to see –
   that what these two inherit now
   is an aftermath which may grow
   crime upon endless crime?
   (*He turns into the sun's rays*)
   Oh, for the warm virgin soil
   where Adam took the gift of life
   without toil – without one stain;
   for how can we redeem by toil
   all these generations of shame?
   (*Looking off up fjord path*)

(*Bitterly*) Here come our 'sons of toil' –
all too ready to be redeemed – so long as no one asks of them
the least sacrifice!

Some men from the village come into view round the cliff. A FISHERMAN
– the spokesman – comes forward towards BRAND. *He carries a*
package.

FISHERMAN (*a little shame-faced*):
We scarce thought to see you alive again.
Is he gone?

BRAND: The fisherman? – Yes.

FISHERMAN: Oh! (*Doffing cap*) Well, you've helped him on his
way.
Here's a bit of food for the other two.
Sheriff gave it us. Will you give it to them?

BRAND: When called to cross the fjord with me,
a greater gift was asked of you.

(*Turning away*)

Give every gift, yet grudge you life,
and gifts are as worthless as Abraham's knife
without his will.

FISHERMAN: Abraham's knife without . . . Yes, maybe;
but we are just simple folk – just sons of toil.

BRAND: If you haven't the heart to reach up for God's crown
don't chafe at the yoke which bows you down –
so conveniently.

FISHERMAN: Yoke . . . Uhu!
But we thought that such as you
might tell us how to throw that yoke away.

BRAND: If you could, I would.

FISHERMAN: You could make us.

BRAND: I? No.

FISHERMAN: But the way you crossed that wild water! Oh –
It was worth a book of sermons, sir.
And now we are asking you to be ours;
for it's you we need.

BRAND: For what? (*Uneasily*)

FISHERMAN: For what?
Why, for the pastor, here in the fjord.

> *Murmur of support from others.*

BRAND: I? – pastor? *here?*

FISHERMAN: We've had no pastor this three years.

BRAND: I am already called to a greater task.
Besides, where rocks shut out the sky
tongues have no power.

FISHERMAN (*quickly*): The rocks multiply
a calling voice – in echoes, sir.

BRAND: Stand aside.

FISHERMAN (*doggedly*): No. Listen to me.
This other call that you can't give up,
is it all that precious to you, pastor?

BRAND: It is my very *life*. (*Passionately*)

FISHERMAN: Your *Life*? (*Slyly*) Then you must stay.

BRAND: Why?

FISHERMAN: Give every gift, yet grudge your *life*,
and gifts are as worthless as . . . as Abraham's knife
without his will.

> *Murmur of approval from the other men.*

BRAND: One gift a man dares not give,
is the mission by which his soul must live;
for to dam up the river of the soul
is to watch life wither where it grew.

FISHERMAN: Yet bury your river in a dark hole,
and it still can reach the sea, as dew.

BRAND: Who puts words in your mouth?

FISHERMAN (*quickly*): Why you.
When the storm was up and raging, sir,
and you sailed, risking life and limb,
for the sake of that poor sinner in there;
when you upped with your pennant in the wild air,
you hoisted my soul. Tomorrow – who knows – (*Slyly*)
I might haul it down, just because
I can't seem to keep it up and still do
the day's work too.

BRAND: If you *will* not be what God made you for,
then be whole-heartedly what you are –
sons of toil. (*Brushing past him*)

FISHERMAN: Then, woe unto you! For you throw at our heads
a lamp we could not light, my son.
And woe unto us, who for one day
saw its light shine! (*Murmur of assent*)
Come, brothers! We've asked in vain.
So we must back into the shadows again.

The FISHERMAN *turns, joins his fellows and they all go silently back
down the path which leads to the fjord.*

BRAND: Oh, take me out of this coffin of despair,
to where my heart has room to beat!

(*Seeing* AGNES)

You sit there as though your quiet power
generated the sun around your hair.

She does not seem to hear.

He approaches her.

C

Is it the fjord winding out to sea
which holds your eyes as if eyes could hear?
For sight is wasted on a clear sky.

AGNES (*without turning – still staring off*):
No, not the fjord, nor this earth –
But in the sky I seem to see
the landscape of some greater earth –
a country of my inmost dreams.

(*As in a trance*)

Oceans I see, and mouths of streams
echoing sunlight through the mists;
while, beyond the mountain crests,
sunbleached deserts I see where
huge palms, switching with the winds,
agitate – like widows' hands –
the flat, black shadows. In the air
no bird flies; no life is there.
And yet there *are* voices singing,
and the words . . . (*Listening*) the words –

BRAND (*troubled by her vision*): . . . Yes?

AGNES: – Forever lose or save your soul!
See your dread task! Hear your high call!
Oh, Brand, Brand – Bring to birth
the new people for the new earth!

BRAND (*uneasily*): What else?

AGNES: Now I feel . . .
I feel my own heart fill and swell,
like rivers rising as they run,
and still the voices through the sun –
For the new earth make the new man!
And now I sense, more than I see,
Him, who hovers over all –
sense his eyes as they fall,
full of charity yet full
of utter sadness. The face is kind,
and yet in his eyes I seem to see
the child he sacrificed for me.

And again the singing voices cry
Work! Work and bring to birth
the new man for this new earth!
Oh, Brand, Brand, my heart is so full!

BRAND (*turning away, amazed*): In the heart.
Through the heart. There lies the way!
There, in its first fertility,
is Adam's earth – the virgin soil.
Not on the horizons of the world
but here – in the heart of man.
But the will? –

As his eye catches someone moving up from the fjord.

Who is this woman? so old, yet so—— Oh—— (*Troubled*)
How like a vulture's her crooked neck. No:

(*As though dismissing an idea*)

Yet, her talon fingers fumble in
her placket pockets, as if a deep sin
swung untouchable treasures there.
Round withered hands the long skirt hangs
like folds of feathered skin; like tongs,
her hands have arms,
– the hawk?

(*Suddenly disturbed*)

Oh – What chill memories are set astir
from my childhood now? There comes from her
a cold frost which grips my throat,
an heart's avalanche, which will smother
hope with fear . . . ? Dear God! . . . My mother.

Coming into view from the fjord, BRAND'S MOTHER *stands, and,
shading her eyes, peers around.*

MOTHER: Where is he? Drat the sun out here!
It will take all the eyesight left me! There!
Son, is that you?

BRAND: It is.

MOTHER (*rubbing her eyes*): I still can't make out if it's priest or
beast. (*Chuckles*)

BRAND: Sunlight didn't trouble us at home.

MOTHER: No. It's a good gloom, son. Eh? Eh? Son? Where's
 your tongue?

BRAND: Mother, I cannot stop to talk.

MOTHER: You were always one to get away.

BRAND: Did it break your heart?

MOTHER: I can't say it did.
 I had good reason to get you away –
 to become a priest. And now, look at you!
 Broad and strong, too. But reckless. Eh? Oh!
 I heard what you did. Crossing the fjord!
 Are you trying to throw your life away?
 You – the last of our line – my flesh and my bone!
 and God knows how soon – my heir.

BRAND: I see.
 And is that why you come seeking me,
 with your pockets bulging? Is my inheritance there?

He touches her with his staff.

MOTHER (*recoiling violently*): What? Stand away!
 Stop where you are; or I'll use my stick on you!
 Ah! Son! Don't let us quarrel again.
 I'm not getting younger as the years pass.
 And very soon *all* I possess
 will be yours. But I tell you now,
 it's all at home. I have nothing on me.
 Laid out in neat bundles it lies.
 Keep away! I shan't hide your inheritance from you.
 It will all be there, laid out for you –
 on the day I die.

BRAND: On what conditions?

MOTHER: Oh – Just one:
 that you will not throw your life away
 on some reckless, thankless, fruitless task:
 that you'll tend to – and add to – the family tree,
 child by child. That is all.
 And as for your new inheritance.

If you cannot make it more,
shut it up safe and lock the door –
till you breed brats of my kind.

(*Chuckles*)

BRAND (*coming a step nearer to her*):
And what if I did have a mind
to scatter it to the four winds!

MOTHER: Scatter!
What took me my life to collect?
What broke my back and made my hair grey?
Scatter?

BRAND: Scatter, – like bread upon the sea.

MOTHER: Son, if you scatter my fortune abroad,
you scatter my soul. You would not dare.

BRAND (*watching her closely*):
Yet, what if I did? What if one night soon
I stand by the oblong where
the white wax tapers hem *you* in;
and these hands, shrivelled and thin,
clasp the prayer-book from which prayer
never more may purpose breath:
if, sleeping *your* first night of death,
I come stealing, fumbling, feeling;
groping till the treasure's found;
if bit by bit I draw it out;
if taking up the wax light I . . .

MOTHER: . . . Stop!!
(*Coming nearer to him, tensely*)
Where do you get such a nightmare from?

BRAND: Where? Need I tell *you*?
That autumn night that father died.
You were said to be sick all day.
So, I sneaked in to where he lay
as pale as soap in the candlelight,
then stopped and stood, in awe of his face
in the final sleep. In that shadowy place,

I noted the smell of unaired sheets;
and how his fingers held the Book,
though his wrists were slim and weak;
and then I heard steps on the stair;
and a woman came in.

The MOTHER starts.

                              She could not see me.
So, stealing up to where he lay,
she felt around, then rummaged in the bed;
then she shifted the dead man's head;
then drew out a fat bundle of notes;
then others, muttering, more and more!

Then plunging her arm in the pillow slip,
she pulled out a packet at which she tore
with feverish fingers, but, as it held,
took her *teeth* to it! till it spilled
gold on the floor. She swooped on her prey,
again and again, till the bundles all
gave up their gold and discarded fell
like carcasses. Then, like a lost soul
inheriting the burden on its back,
she slunk from the room, stooped under a sack,
and in going moaned, 'and that was all!'

MOTHER (*slowly*):
The need was great which made that gain small.
I had paid a price you cannot understand.
Your grandfather married me to a man
with a withered old body – because of his land.
Don't think that I walked as meek as a lamb
from the lad in the village I'd always loved.
It was a bad bargain – even in cash.
But since then I've kept my hand to the plough,
and doubled the sum.

BRAND: And was it not rash
to double the sum at the double cost
of a soiled body and a soul lost
so near the grave?

MOTHER: Not rash; which I prove
by your presence and the cloth you wear.
When my time comes you'll be there,
my own priest –

BRAND: I see. And the debt?

MOTHER: Debt? What debt? I have no debts.

BRAND: Have you not rather squandered the loan
God gave you, when He gave you a soul?

MOTHER: ... Soul? But ...

BRAND: Oh, don't be afraid.
I will redeem your debt by my deeds.
You'll rest without debt.

MOTHER: Without debt or sin.

BRAND: (*facing her*):
I will take over your debt; but your sin, –
His spirit, starved in that withered frame,
like a dove caged in a prison of bone –
that you yourself must explain;
or even yet, repenting, release
his prisoner spirit, and go in the peace
of his compassion.
                    (*Quietly*) Repent, or perish.

MOTHER (*Uneasily*):
I'll get back to the honest gloom under my cliff.
This sunshine here breeds unhealthy notions.
(*Scathingly*) A dove caged in a prison of bone!

(*She makes to go*)

BRAND: Mother! – If you need me I shall come.

MOTHER: Yes. With your judgments, priest. (*As she goes*)

BRAND: No, as your son –
not to condemn, but to shield you from
other judgment. Then, Mother, I'll sing
songs by your bed, whose love will ring
joyous echoes from these rocks.

MOTHER: You will? (*Incredulously*) Will you swear that by The
   Cross? Eh?

BRAND: Yes, when you repent, I'll come.
   But *I* must make one condition too.

MOTHER: Yes?

BRAND: That all that binds you to the earth –
   all monies and goods you must . . .

MOTHER: Yes?

BRAND: – *renounce.*
   And go down naked as at birth
   to the grave's encounter.

MOTHER: What!? – Son . . . no!
   Son, I'll put silver and gold in the box,
   when I next go to church.

BRAND: All you have?

MOTHER: Is plenty, not enough?

BRAND: Nothing less than *all* will do.

MOTHER: My life wasted! My soul condemned,
   and my wealth dismissed with a wave of the hand!
   If that's the way of it, let me get home
   and nurse what I still can call my own;
   my joy, my treasure, my golden boy!

            (*Nursing what's hidden in her skirt pocket*)

   Then how is it – priest – that my soul had to borrow
   this flesh, if the needs of the flesh destroy
   the soul itself? Don't desert me. (*Turning back*)
   Stay near. Who knows what my mind may be
   when the hour comes. If I gave away.
   Or perhaps if I spend . . .
   No! I'll hang on to it; till the bitter end.

      The MOTHER *goes back down into the shadows.*

BRAND (*watching her go*): Yes Mother – so your priest must
remain, till, dying and contrite, you send for him.

BRAND *stands looking back into the fjord.*

AGNES (*who is still sitting on the rock*) :
Oh! Brand! The sky!
See how the setting sun has made
a world of islands in the red cloud.

BRAND : Yes. (*Turning and moving to her*) So much for my defiant
dawn; my evening's meek.

AGNES : The evening, for me, is better than the morning.

BRAND : Not for me. (*He watches the sunset*)
Dreams of glory – swans of dreams –
came in flocks across my brain.
My path led on and outwards to
new horizons. But now, from these rocks,
I look back into this abyss
where long before the sun's in the sea
darkness has come, and it calls to me.
All the day's glories overhead die,
narrowed to one ribbon of sky – (*Turning to* AGNES)
for, the call must be answered. And this is my call:
to fight my own people – fight for their soul!

AGNES : And the old God, who was to fall?

BRAND : He will still be seen to his grave;
But not with any flourish now.
I was wrong. No gift of mine,
no growth of talent, virtue or skill,
is the hope of the world: it is The Will –
the will to become God's creature again.
For it is His Will that we regain
the primal Adam, who was in His sight
the tablet whereon He should write
the characters of Heaven.

EINAR *comes in by the path from the fjord.*

EINAR: Brand – (*awkwardly*) Where is she?

BRAND: There she sits.

EINAR(*going to* AGNES *hesitantly*): Agnes
– I was afraid – not of losing my life but of losing you.
I never dreamed that you would go.
Why *did* you go? Answer me.
Is it him with his talk? Agnes, you must answer me.
Can he already mean more to you than I do?

(She does not answer)

Then you must choose between us . . . and now.
For, when the steamer goes
I go too. Make your choice.

AGNES (*quietly*): But I have no choice.

EINAR (*incredulously*): Agnes!

AGNES: Greet my brothers – my sisters – my mother.
Say I shall write – if the words come.

EINAR: But this is madness! You can't just leave me now.

AGNES: Einar, I must. (*Quietly*) I will.

BRAND (*amazed yet troubled*): Girl, be sure.
Cramped here between fjord and fell –
shadowed over by cliffs and snow –
you'd live like a rockbird on a ledge.
Life would be the perpetual grey
of twilight on a November day.

AGNES: Lack of light does not frighten me –
now that a new earth shines in our sky.

BRAND: Remember – my demands are hard.
What my soul asks of me – and of mine –
is *All* or *Nothing*. There's no safeguard –
no haggling conditions – no humane design,
where life itself may not be too dear
to pay for God's will working through mine.

EINAR: Agnes! Get clear of this madman.
Let his benighted soul alone.
Cling to a life which is your own,
and leave him with his cliffs and mews
to moan Salvation!

BRAND (*simply, to* AGNES): Where the roads cross . . . choose.

BRAND goes by the path to the fjord.

EINAR (*desperately*):
Choose between his way and my way.
Choose between night and day.
Choose between suffocation and breath.
Choose between life and *death*!

AGNES (*calmly*):
Through death, if it must be. (*She rises*)
For *through* the night is the one way on
towards the new light . . . (*moving away*) . . . of dawn.

AGNES goes, following after BRAND.

EINAR gazes after her, as the light goes from the day.

CURTAIN

ACT TWO

Scene 1

Three years later.

A small garden at the side of the pastor's house.

The house is built under an overhang of rock and on a shelf of the cliff above the fjord. Beyond the gate is a path which leads down to where the old church and some of the houses of the village stand. There is a bench in the garden.

The atmosphere is chill and it is late afternoon.

BRAND *stands, looking down the path while* AGNES *sits on the steps mending a child's garment.*

AGNES: Are you expecting someone?

BRAND: Yes, (*still looking out*) word from my mother.

AGNES: I am glad.

BRAND: Not more than I. (*Turning to her*) For three years I have hoped that she'd send for me. Now I am told she is nearing her end.

AGNES: Brand, (*gently*) – shouldn't you go right away, without waiting for word?

BRAND: Without her repentance, no words of mine can bring her any real peace.

AGNES: You are hard – so hard.

BRAND: To you too?

AGNES: Oh no – not to me! – mostly to yourself.

BRAND (*moving restlessly about*): I said it would be a hard life here, but how could you know what it would be on this rock-shelf, in the biting winds, with solid rock above our heads?

AGNES: But I like the hood of rock overhead. It makes me feel safe.

BRAND: Safe?

AGNES: Yes, and most of all in the Spring.

BRAND: In the Spring?

AGNES: Yes. (*Happily*)
When all the buds below become green,
and the glacier up above in the sun
moves down its annual inch. For then
the avalanches come thundering down,
and only shoot over our heads and go
splash into the fjord below.
Then it seems to me as if we three
were the green plants which always grow
behind a waterfall.

BRAND: Grow? (*Almost to self*) But how can plants continue to grow without the sun?

AGNES: But they must. They do. (*Troubled*) Don't they?

BRAND (*avoiding her eye*): A sunless home is a dreadful thing. And when the child's blue eyes can only see the Spring sun dancing over there, on the inaccessible side of the fjord, will he not grow as I grew – hard? But he's a more delicate thing and . . . Oh! why is there no word from her? (*Watching path*)

AGNES: Brand, you have a special fear of this lack of sun. Haven't you?

BRAND: Haven't you?

AGNES: Sometimes I do worry about him. So many other children just waste away.

BRAND (*with more will than heart*): Oh, but he couldn't be taken from us! God is good! No, no! In the end – wait till you see – he'll grow up the biggest, strongest boy . . . Where is he now?

AGNES: Inside. In his cot.

BRAND (*pushing door ajar*): Look! (*Whispering*) His hand is reached out above the cot. But he's asleep.

AGNES: His hands too are thin.

BRAND: Yes, but you are over-anxious. (*With forced confidence*) Let
him sleep and he'll grow strong again. (*Closing door gently*) Sleep,
and God guard you, my son. Agnes, with the coming of the
child success has attended all I've done.

AGNES: You have deserved your success.

BRAND (*tenderly*): It was easy – because of you.

AGNES: It was your love for people that brought success. The
key was here – in your heart.

BRAND: You unlocked my heart and set it free.
For no man can open his heart to love all,
until he first has loved one soul
To the heart's fullness.
(*He kisses her head as she sews*)

AGNES (*Looking up as he moves restlessly about again*):
Yet, Brand, your love is a difficult love.
And there are many who have turned away,
unable to face your demand
of *All* or *Nothing*.

BRAND: Agnes, did He –
when the Son of Man in agony kneeled,
and prayed 'Oh, take this cup away!' –
did He then stand as a fatherly shield
between that passion and that cup?

As she does not answer.

No. The crown of life does not fall
to a compromise. We must give *all*.
That we *cannot* do so He will forgive;
but that we *will* not – that sin might live
to visit at our own child's door.

AGNES: But, for the child's sake may not we
be forgiven some little compromise?

BRAND (*sadly and deliberately*):
   One wilful compromise where we withhold
   belief from its action, and we have told
   God the unforgivable lie.

AGNES (*rising and embracing him*): Go where you must. I will
   follow you.

BRAND (*smiling*): No climb was ever too steep for two.

He kisses her.

The DOCTOR *coming down the path stops at the gate, seeing them in each
other's arms.*

DOCTOR (*leaning on wall*): Can turtle doves really exist among
   these Godforsaken rocks!

AGNES: Doctor! My dear old Doctor! (*She runs to the gate*) Fancy
   you being here! Why Doctor, the last time I saw you . . . (*She
   stops*)

DOCTOR: Yes, (*nodding*) the last time you saw me was at your
   engagement party – to *Einar*. Well at least he was going to carry
   you off to climes more suiting your delicate health (*shivering*) –
   certainly warmer!

The DOCTOR *comes inside the gate.*

AGNES: Come right inside. You've not seen the baby yet.

DOCTOR: No, I'll not come in. (*And aside to her*)
   You know well enough that I'm still angry with you,
   for tying yourself to him and this place –
   where the winter winds cut through flesh and soul.

BRAND (*coming forward*): Not through the soul, Doctor.

DOCTOR: No? (*Turning to face him*) At any rate I can't stay.
   I have a patient expecting me down by the point.

BRAND: My mother?

DOCTOR: Yes. Coming along? (*Noticing* AGNES *dropping her eyes*)
   Or have you been?

BRAND: No. She sent for you. Till she sends for me
   I can do nothing, Doctor, but pray
   that that summons will come.

DOCTOR (*to* AGNES): Lord help you, child!
　– in such pitiless hands as these.

BRAND: I am not pitiless.

AGNES: Oh no, Doctor!
　He would give his own life to wash away
　her debt to Heaven.

DOCTOR: *Her* debt to Heaven?
　Let him first clear his own debts towards humanity! Good-day!

The DOCTOR *moves to the gate.*

BRAND: In the sight of God, *all* debts
　can be atoned for by the acts of one!

DOCTOR (*turning angrily at gate*): Well, not by one
　who in the matter of charity
　is a very beggar!——

BRAND (*interrupting*): – beggared or rich
　– I will what I will, with all my soul,
　and that pure will embraces all!

DOCTOR: Will! (*With grim irony*) Will, Pastor?
　But don't your precious powers above
　also advocate ... Love!

The DOCTOR *slams the gate and goes.*

AGNES: Doctor! (*In distress, as he goes*)

BRAND: Love!
　There is no word so abused to-day,
　as this word Love.
　If one falls by the way,
　because that way is long and sheer,
　there is a short-cut none need fear
　– through *Love*.
　If a man has sipped the cup of life dry,
　still – he can always try
　this – *Love*.
　Or should he sight his goal but feel
　the strife to reach that point above

rather beyond him – why!
there is *Love*.
And, lastly, at the end of his time,
cringing in pity and steeped in crime,
he dares appeal the powers above,
in hope of the Repeal Through *Love*.

AGNES: Then is all love weakness?

BRAND: No! (*Ardently*) No!
But what most people refuse to see
is that great *will* must precede great love.
For to hang on The Cross in agony
is nothing. But to have *willed* it so –
(*Turning away*) that was the love of Calvary.
Here, where Tolerance apes Love,
true Love must often seem like hate . . . Ah! –

A MAN *comes breathlessly through the gate.*

MAN: Pastor! – you're wanted down there at once.

BRAND (*eagerly*): Did my mother send some message with you?

MAN: Yes. It's a strange one too. She raised herself up on the bed,
and then she whispered in my ear, 'Fetch priest, and tell him
from me, for the sacrament – half my property.'

BRAND: God!

MAN: That's what she said.

BRAND: Then go back and say that this is the message the priest
has sent – 'Neither priest, nor sacrament may come for half
measures.'

MAN: It was your *mother* who sent for you. You understand?

BRAND: It is for her as for all the rest – *All* or *Nothing*.

MAN (*worried*): That's hard, sir. And for *her* to be giving away
half . . .

BRAND (*interrupting*): . . . Tell her the hoof of the Golden Calf is as
much an idol as the whole beast!

D

MAN: I'll try to soften the blow for her. But there is one thing certain sure – God is not so hard as you are.

MAN goes to gate.

BRAND: Again that Old Man! – The Tolerant God!

A SECOND MAN meets the other at the gate.

MAN: Pastor, sir!

BRAND: Yes? What's your message?

2ND MAN: Your mother says to tell you now that she is willing give away almost all of her property if only you . . .

BRAND: She cannot bargain for her soul! *That* man has my reply.

The TWO MEN whisper.

2ND MAN: But she's in pain, and desperate you'll come.

1ST MAN: Sir, it's a mother calling her son.

BRAND (*in great distress*): Shall I then measure others by standards which I dare not apply when it comes to my own flesh and blood?

2ND MAN: She'll not give in and you know it too.

1ST MAN: At least you can show her some mercy at the end.

BRAND: Tell her the message I gave you. Go! The bread and the wine of mercy require a clean table. (*As they hesitate*) Go! Do you hear!

The TWO MEN go, muttering.

AGNES (*quietly*): Brand, the conditions you impose are impossibly hard.

BRAND: With my aims ask milder if you dare.
For those who'd be raised up from here
there can only be some kind of cross.
      (*He turns to her, his voice almost breaking*)
Yet when I have faced some frightened soul
and dared to demand that he should so rise,
his hurt eyes swimming in my eyes

have made of our common tears a sea,
where even I clutch wreckage and . . .
long for God's outreached hand.
Then I've bitten my tongue which made the demand
and wept in agony, wanting to take
that soul in my arms, for pity's sake.

> AGNES *coming near to him he takes her in his arms.*

Oh, Agnes! Agnes.

> (*Having recovered composure*)

See to the child.
Guide him into deeper dreams.
For a sleeping child seems to lie in a lake,
above whose calm surface a mother may skim –
like a soundless bird – yet in his dream
her love be mirrored. (*Sighing*)
                         That surface men break.

AGNES: Wherever your thoughts fly they come back to the child.
   What is it?

BRAND: Nothing. Nothing. Go quietly in. (*Opening door*) He's
   still asleep.

AGNES (*whispered*): Give me some thought to strengthen me.

BRAND (*whispered*): He who is guiltless – he shall live.

AGNES: He is our one treasure God dares not claim.

> AGNES *goes in.*

BRAND: Yet, if God did dare?
   If my own son were made Isaac to my Abraham's dread?

> *As the* SHERIFF *comes to the gate.*

SHERIFF: Good afternoon, Pastor! (*Brightly*)

BRAND: Good afternoon, Sheriff. (*Uncertainly*)

SHERIFF (*dryly*): It's not often I'm up this way,
   and perhaps a visit from me to-day
   might seem ill-timed, eh?

BRAND : If you have something to say to me, come in off the path.
  (*Letting* SHERIFF *in gate.*)
  Well, Sheriff what is it?

SHERIFF : They tell me your mother's bad. That's bad.

BRAND : It is about that you came?

SHERIFF (*hesitantly*): Well——in a way.
  But, seeing as I was passing by –
  or almost – I thought to myself, thought I,
  as well jump as crawl. Eh?

BRAND : I didn't say anything.

SHERIFF : No. Well I'll straight to the point.
  When your mother's gone – and she might go to-day –
  you will be wealthy.

BRAND (*turning away*): I see. So you think I'll be wealthy?

SHERIFF (*following it up*): I don't *think* – I know.
  Doesn't she own all the land
  of every fjord that one can see
  from the top of that path? Eh?
  Pastor, trust me, you're rolling in wealth –
  So long as she doesn't recover her health. Ha!
  (*About to laugh*) We know there was no love lost – I mean –
  Well, here was I thinking – just to-day –
  when he becomes a man of means
  he won't be over anxious to stay
  in this depressing and out-of-the-way
  ditch of a parish. Eh?

BRAND (*turning to face him*): Sheriff.

SHERIFF :   Yes?

BRAND : Is the gist of your present errand to me not simply –
  Go away!?

SHERIFF (*taking a big breath and plunging*): Yes, it is.
Honestly – Pastor, just cast your eye
on the sort of folk that you now try
to raise to an understanding of
the finer points of Theology.
You deserve a bigger community.

BRAND: His home soil beneath a man's feet
is as the roots to a growing tree.

SHERIFF: Mm!
That's the very sort of words I mean –
for educated folk with some brain –
but not for us poor fisherfolk.
It's poetical. Oh! when one's tired,
and the day's work done, one may be inspired
by a modicum of poetry.
But not too much. My motto's Thrift.
Yes – even in matter of uplift. (*Smiling*)
And that's where we differ – you and I –
you want your uplift every day.
Am I not right when I say,
that you would unite Religion and Life:
make one-and-the same-thing of God's strife
and the struggle for potatoes? Eh?

BRAND: If you choose to put it that way – yes.

SHERIFF: Well, for the people here that's not the way.
I'm a man of the people and I know.
I have fought for the rights of the peasant here,
foot by foot, year by year.
I have introduced new branches of trade,
and everything going smoothly ahead,
by adding this and that attraction –
and Nature defeated by road and bridge.

BRAND (*interrupting*): Not the bridge between belief and action?

SHERIFF (*annoyed*): – Between the uplands and the fjord.

BRAND: Not between Life and The Word.

SHERIFF (*rather exasperated*):
Be practical, Pastor!
First get communications going.
First get roads between door and door.
There were no two opinions on that before;
but now the whole issue has been confused!
You have split in two camps the folk I had fused
into one great united front!
We must march with the times. And you too. But not here.

BRAND: My work is here. And here I stay.

SHERIFF: Well, all I can say (*threateningly*)
is keep to your side of the fence.
Just don't you let your work spread
as if God made the potato bread,
and the Almighty Himself was on board
of every boat that sailed the fjord!

BRAND (*quietly*): I have lighted a lamp for all who live here,
and I will keep it shining until one day,
when I break the spell under which they grew
unable to rise because of *you*, –
with your dictatorship of things.

(*Simply*)

And on that day when my bell rings,
if you dare oppose what its tongue sings
it will be war.

SHERIFF: If you dare start your war from this rock-
shelf, who'll be the first to fall? – yourself.

BRAND: Yet I do dare.

SHERIFF: Death and Destruction, man!
I've seen parson after parson breaking down.
Now you're on the verge. Go south while you can.

BRAND: Here I belong.

SHERIFF: But think what you have to lose!
a wife – a child – your mother's gold.

BRAND: I lose myself if I give in.

SHERIFF: Very well! (*Making for the gate*)
    But the lone soldier cannot win.

BRAND: On my side I will have the best.

SHERIFF: Yes – (*Turning at the gate*)
    but on mine I'll have the *most*!

The SHERIFF *goes.*

BRAND: A man of the people – and the people's pest!
    No avalanche, famine, flood or frost
    works half the havoc wrought by him
    in any one year.
    Oh (*Looking down path*) He's met the Doctor.

He goes to meet the DOCTOR *at the gate.*

Well?

The DOCTOR *does not answer, but comes on in.*

My mother . . . ?

DOCTOR (*slowly*): She now stands before one who has the right to
    judge her, my son.

For a moment BRAND *is too shocked to speak, and when he does, it is
    with difficulty.*

BRAND: Did she . . . repent?

DOCTOR: Repent? No! (*Scornfully*)

BRAND: Did she say anything?

DOCTOR: Oh yes. At the very last . . . 'God has not so hard a
    fist as my son.'

BRAND *sinks on to the bench.*

BRAND: Even in death's agony, the same self-destroying lie,
    of the tolerant God!
    Another soul lost! Her soul lost too!

DOCTOR (*looking down at* BRAND):
All this talk of lost souls, my son,
belongs to an age now dead and gone.
You can't hold up Time, and our age won't be
scared into Heaven by Hellfire. To-day,
for us who are strong, healthy, and sane,
one commandment is enough – Be humane!

BRAND: Humane!
That supine word corrupts mankind!
Was God humane to Jesus Christ?
Why! – if your God, who is feeble and kind,
had been allowed to have His way
Christ had cried mercy from the cross
and climbed down and crept away! Ah! . . .

Burying his head in his hands.

AGNES *comes from the house.*

DOCTOR (*gently to* BRAND): Give the storm way. If you could
bring yourself to tears it would not do you any harm.

AGNES (*approaching* DOCTOR – *whispers*): Doctor, in here. Follow
me.

DOCTOR (*startled*): Why, what is it, child?

AGNES: In God's name come!

AGNES *and* DOCTOR *go into house.* BRAND *sits alone.*

BRAND: So, another debt is passed on – from the parent to the
son.

The DOCTOR *comes from house with* AGNES.

DOCTOR (*To* AGNES): No doubt about it. I know the signs. Put
your own house in order, Brand! The sooner you go from
here the better.

BRAND: I cannot now ever move from here.

DOCTOR: Then answer for your child's life!

BRAND: My child's life? Agnes! (*He makes for the house door*)

DOCTOR: Wait! (*Restraining him*) He's not in immediate danger now. But it is as Agnes feared: another few weeks in this sunless place will kill such a delicate little soul. The money shouldn't be wanting now, so go south with him as soon as you can. The sooner the better, and if I were you to-morrow wouldn't be soon enough.

BRAND: To-morrow? He'll go from this house to-night. Oh! (*Distracted*) My mother. Now him. But *he* cannot die! Agnes, he *must* not. (*Turning to her*)

AGNES: No, Brand, he'll not die. We'll go away.

BRAND (*turning to the* DOCTOR): Doctor, can you promise me that that if we go it *will* save him?

DOCTOR: I believe it will.

BRAND (*Turning to her*): Agnes, get him wrapped up now – and a few things together and——

AGNES: Now? (*Surprised*) But——

BRAND (*hardly heeding her*): It's such a bitter wind. Put on the new coat – the one with the swansdown hood. What are you waiting for?

AGNES: But, now? To-night?

BRAND: Yes, yes. To-night we'll take him down to the harbour-master's house. To-morrow we shall get the steamer. I have friends in the south. I'll not have him stay another night in this coffin of a house! Go, woman! Go!

AGNES *goes in while* BRAND *turns away thinking feverishly.*

DOCTOR (*crossing over to* BRAND):
For the world *All* or *Nothing*, my son;
but, when one *is* the world, then,
the *little* or *much* of compassion counts.
Yes – One learns from personal suffering.

BRAND: What do you mean?

DOCTOR: Well—— To your mother, no pity at all –
all your goods or nothing. *All!*
To the people in distress, the same.
But now that the distress is yours
dare you now to label it shame –
this saving of life – this being *humane*?
No parson preoccupied with the soul,
but a father now!

BRAND: Oh! Am I blind?
Or have I been blind up till now?

DOCTOR: In my eyes, with your wings clipped, son,
you are greater now than that great man
you imagined you were. Fare-you-well!
Now I have passed you the looking-glass,
look in it. It can do no harm,
to sigh and say, 'That is the face
of Brand, who was to take Heaven by storm.'
I must get back before sunset! Good-luck! – in the South

The DOCTOR *goes out and back up the path by which he had come.*

BRAND (*staring straight in front of him*): Then or now – when was I
wrong?

AGNES *comes out of the door with her cloak over her shoulders, a bag in
her hand and the child wrapped up in her arms.* BRAND *does not see her.
She is going to speak when she sees the expression on his face and seems
speechless in terror. Finally she approaches him.*

AGNES: I am ready.

BRAND (*staring at her*): Ready? Ready? But what for?

AGNES: Brand!——

Suddenly GERD *runs past clapping her hands and shouting, then comes to
the gate.*

GERD (*approaching*): Have you heard the news? Have you heard
the news? Parson's off on the back of the hawk! And all the
parish devils are loosed!

BRAND: What brings *her* here now? Gerd——

GERD: Parson's off on the hawk's back.

BRAND (*calling*): Gerd! Here I am. I have not gone.

GERD: Ha, you! But not the priest. No. (*Leaping on the wall*)
I saw it swoop! I saw him go!
Down from the Ice-Church came the hawk –
rushing, swishing through the dusk;
swept across the tusks of rock,
across the bog, like hissing talk
of rumours whispered in the dark –
Down! Down! – and into that kirk. (*Pointing*)
Then saddled and bridled, back it flew,
and there on its back a man I knew.
It was the priest! The priest! Not you!

(*Coming into the garden*)

Up there in my church he stands,
while icicles drip from his hands.
His thick white robes have edges pearled
with frosted drops, his lace is snow;
and what he is going to preach, I know
will shock the whole world – (*with rising voice*)
shock it so!!

BRAND *stands over her.*

BRAND: What brought you from the snows now
with talk of idols?

GERD: Idols? How?
Idols? Oh! I know what you mean!
gilded, painted, and pretty all –
pretty! Have you an idol? Eh?
What's that wrapped up in a shawl? (*To* AGNES)
Is it a doll? Is it a doll?
Or is it – *an idol*? Ha! (*Dances with joy*)

AGNES: Oh, now I see that desert where
the palms hung blackened by the sun.
But the voices no longer cry. We are lost, Brand. Lost!

BRAND: Agnes!

GERD (*suddenly stopping dancing*): Sh! Sh!...
Listen! Listen! All the ice-bells
are pealing from the pinnacles.
And look! From the bog and up the fells
my priest's congregation crawls! (*Voice rising*)
See! All the dead, devil-soul
Pastor ploughed back into the soil
and sealed beneath the crust he'd built
over the black pie of guilt!
Life! Life was let loose to-day
when the hawk carried the priest away!
Down! Down! Down! Then away!

GERD *goes*, *leaping over the wall and crying till her voice is lost in the* *echoes.* (*Off*) The hawk! The hawk! The hawk!

For a moment there is dead silence. Then AGNES *turns to* BRAND.

AGNES (*quietly and fearfully*): We must not hesitate now, but go.

BRAND (*torn with doubts*): Go?

AGNES: Brand! Your child! Your own child!

BRAND: Before I was father was not I pastor here?

AGNES: Yes, I know. But now——

BRAND:——Now as then.

AGNES: But surely a father's first wish
is to save his child – his own son?

BRAND: Abraham wished to save his son.
Yet not his wish, but his will
held him to the trust which sent
the ram crashing through the bush
to let God live in the event.

AGNES: I dare not trust my faith so far.
I must take him away. I must save him! I *must*!

AGNES *moves to the gate.*

BRAND: You must do as a mother should. And I –
as a man ——

AGNES: No (*Turning*) How can I leave you?
Before I was a mother was not I
your wife. Can I leave you here to die –
for this terrible struggle will kill you;
whatever your strength! Oh, be kind, and come.

BRAND: It's not the child's life, not yours, not mine,
which is at stake, Agnes, in this –
but the life of God and its divine
dependence on the will of Man.
We may go and *may* save a life we love.
We may stay and save a world from night.
For our will could crack the crust of dark
and let God's light stream in from above.

AGNES (*defeated*): The choice must be your choice.
For I see, yet I dare not understand.

BRAND: Oh! Take this cup of choice from my hand!

AGNES: *I* cannot and remain a mother.
But ask yourself if you have any choice.
In this case can you doubt God's will?

BRAND: Never! There's life and death in your voice.

AGNES: Then go as God directs you.

BRAND: Go?

AGNES: ——from this dreadful place!
Brand? ——

BRAND (*with a terrific effort of will, he shakes his head*):
No. No!

AGNES (*raising the child in her arms*):
God! – If such sacrifice of life
is your demand, then under your knife
I dare thrust my own son!

(*As she turns to the house*)

But show yourself in this nightmare night!

AGNES *goes into the house with the child.*

BRAND(*for a moment stares in front of him and then in agony cries out*):
Christ! Oh, Christ! Send me light!

CURTAIN

SCENE 2

Inside the house – Christmas Eve of the same year.

Sounds of storm are heard before rise of curtain. It is almost dark in the room – which is lit by one candle.

There is a door to the outside, a door to BRAND'S *study and a curtain or door to the other part of the house.*

There is a window with curtains and shutters inside. These are open.

AGNES *stands near a great linen chest by the window. She is handling some baby clothes. She is in mourning.*

Suddenly she starts guiltily as she hears a sound outside. She looks out of the window and then hurriedly and fearfully packs the baby clothes back into the chest. Then she goes to the door.

AGNES: Brand? Is it you?

BRAND *comes in dusting snow from himself.*

Oh, how long it has seemed! (*Helping him off with his cloak*) I
couldn't have faced another night alone.

BRAND: Ah! It's good to come home. (*Comforting her*) But why so
dark? Why, it's lighter outside in the snow.

BRAND *lights another candle.*

BRAND: Come! We mustn't have a dark house on Christmas Eve.
(*Turning to her*) But you are very pale. You don't look well.
You've been brooding on . . . (*Stopping, then with an effort of will
continuing*) . . . on the child.

AGNES: I am just tired. (*Turning away*) But I did brighten up the house a little. See, I hung up a little greenery – just a few pieces. It was all I had. I have tended that evergreen since last year – to decorate his Christmas tree.

She bursts into tears.

BRAND: Come, my dear! Come. Is this honouring the Lord's feast of Christmas? You must find the will to conquer those tears.

AGNES: And have you no tears? Is that bead of moisture in your eye just a snowflake melting?

BRAND: Let us both take courage to go on from the fact that in this we are one – the one weakness and the one strength. But, oh, it was good to be out there.

(*As he gets his boots off, etc. and* AGNES *helps*)

The sea lashed up the rocks in spray; and the gulls rose silently for fear that crying might cost them seconds of care; then hail drummed down on the deck of the boat; the water hissed; the sail in a gust was rent and carried away in the wind. *And*, as every timber shrieked out our fears and eight men crumpled on their oars like corpses on a Viking's bier, I stood at the rudder and I grew – I grew in the courage they had lost and felt God baptise me anew.

AGNES: It is easy for you to face that storm;
but I am shut up in here,
with nothing more active than my own fear
and no worthwhile work.
So what means of expression have I
... except my tears?

BRAND: Agnes, (*Moving to her and taking her hands*)
often my eyes *are* misted too;
and then humility makes me see
God as closer than ever before –
so close he might be inside that door
and I here, standing, longing to throw
myself in His arms – that I might know
what it is to the lost lamb to be found.

AGNES: Brand, see Him always so
   – as the Shepherd – the Comforter.

BRAND: To man He must be
   majesty and power. But to woman He
   is the Comforter. And to *you*
   is given the special grace to see
   glory in mercy. Bring that mercy to me,
   in your clear eyes; and thus we here
   may possess His person both as mercy *and* power.
   The very essence of marriage is this.

He turns again to the window.

And in bringing your light into this dark you
do more than worthwhile work.

AGNES: The nightmare of his last days is still around me.
   Again last night, while you were away,
   he came and stood in my room.
   He did! He tried to reach towards me. (*Feverishly*) Oh!
   He begged for warmth! He was cold!

BRAND: No! Agnes——

AGNES (*hysterically*): The snow is falling on his grave out there
   and he is cold! – cold!

BRAND: Agnes!
   (*Seizing her shoulders*) Look at me!
   The body only lies under the snow. The *child* is in Heaven.

AGNES (*avoiding his eyes*): Body! Child! They are the one thing to
   me.

BRAND: Oh, but Agnes, you know that——

AGNES: Yes, yes, I know. (*Wearily*) I know.
   But you must be patient with me.
   I can be led – not driven. I need comfort now.
   And the God whom you have taught me to know
   is too great to stoop and comfort me.

BRAND: Would it help to have the old God again?——

AGNES: No . . .

BRAND : —— with his aimless tolerance?

AGNES : No!
But your aims are too great for me.
(*In the fever of exhaustion*) Everything now is too great for me:—
your call, your will; the fjord, the fell;
the sorrow, the memory and all the scale
of this dark struggle! And what is it for?
(*Crying out*) The church?
Is it for that ugly little building out there
that my child has died? (*Pointing through window*)

BRAND : Agnes? (*Shocked*)

AGNES (*defiantly*): Your church is too small a thing to contain this
sacrifice.

BRAND : You mean the church as a building – not the living thing?

AGNES : Oh, I don't know what I mean! (*Wearily*) I just mean the
church – your church.

BRAND : But the building is only a symbol of The Church.
And yet, the symbol should reflect the thing –
the symbol should be worthy. (*He looks out of
the window*) Gerd, the mad gypsy girl, first said
it was ugly. It is only the snow blanketing all
its roofs now, which gives it any grace at all.
Agnes! (*He turns*) You have shown me a way of
redeeming more of my mother's debt. I shall build
a great new church with my mother's wealth.

AGNES : A new building?

BRAND : Yes, the old church *is* too small.
But our new church must grow tall
in majesty, glory, grace and scale
in keeping with this sacrifice.
Can't you see how you have been
God's gift of vision to my eyes?
It is through you that I have seen
each step forward from that day
when you saw the new earth in the sky.
Agnes, never, never leave me.

E

AGNES : I shall be your eyes. And you shall see –
but seeing, guide me. For the way
is hard for a woman.

BRAND :   But, Agnes, it is
the way which leads to the greatest gain of all.

AGNES : Yet spur me harshly and I shall fall.

BRAND : A Greater One commands through me.

AGNES : And One of whom you yourself have said,
He does not scorn those who try,
though they lack the strength and the ability.

She lights a candle and prepares to go.

BRAND : True.
Why are you leaving me now?

AGNES : I have to go through into the dark.
Last Christmas – remember? (*Smiling*) – you scolded me
for being extravagant. We had the light
of every candlestick we possess,
and there stood the Christmas tree – bright with toys,
tinsel, trinkets, and greenery.
If God stoops to eavesdropping He will see
that even in sorrow we do not hide away
from His joy. There! Do you see any tears now?

BRAND (*taking her in his arms; then letting her go gently*):
Child, light *all* the candles. Go.
Cast light around you; for you were made so.

AGNES : And build your great church – but let its bell ring
before the Spring.

AGNES *goes out, to the other part of house, leaving the room lit by one
candle.*

BRAND : Willing, in the midst of her grief! The green leaf on the
martyr's fire! Oh! Let me bear the pain for two. My agony be as
you will; but, God, to her be merciful!

There is a knock at the outside door. The SHERIFF *comes in.*

Sheriff? (*Surprised*)

SHERIFF: The snow's driving bad again. I'm sorry, Pastor, to
trouble you on Christmas Eve. But now that our war has come
to a close with you in power, what better day for a peace pact,
eh?

BRAND: A fight like ours has no end. But if need of real peace
brings you ... ?

SHERIFF: Well ... No. It's another endless battle.

BRAND: Oh?

SHERIFF: With the common enemy – Poverty.
You haven't by any chance, Brand,
been misled by Christian charity
into giving shelter to a child
and a runaway gypsy?

BRAND: A gypsy? No.
Is it Gerd you mean?

SHERIFF: Gerd? No.
When I was patrolling the district today
I rounded up a gypsy band:
they're locked up in safe custody
with your next door neighbour. But *one* got away.
I won't sleep till she's under lock and key.

BRAND: And my bell rang out Peace on Earth to-day.

SHERIFF: Well it rang in this lot of devilment too.
And '*keeping* the peace' is up to me.
They're a pest on the land these gypsies, and Oh!
I could tell you a thing or two.
Do you know that it wouldn't be wrong to say
that they're local produce! – your parishioners too!
Yes, (*slyly*) they even have claims on you.

BRAND: On me? – me personally?

SHERIFF: Oh, very personally! Ha!
I'll tell you a riddle before I go –
for I must – but listen closely. Now –

'There are some who spring from where you came,
and yet whose source is not the same.'
Got it?

BRAND (*wearily*): Life is already too full of riddles.

SHERIFF: Ah, but you hold the solution to this one.
Haven't you heard the local story about
the poor parish boy who turned out
a brilliant scholar and courted your mother?

BRAND: No. Why, what happened to him?

SHERIFF: Well, put yourself in your mother's place.
She was the pick of the local queens.
He was poor – she was someone of means;
so they sent him packing.
(*Confidentially*) Do you know what he did?
Half-crazy – after a terrible scene –
he walked out, fell in with a gypsy band
and increased their number before he died,
off a gypsy girl. And now the land
supports so many bastards the more.
Yes, and this parish had to consent
to keeping one – a living monument
to his fine goings-on!

BRAND (*troubled*): And who is this one?

SHERIFF: Do you mean to tell me you've never heard?
The mad gypsy brat of course——

BRAND: Gerd?

SHERIFF: Yes ... Gerd. See the riddle now?
His brats came because of her,
from whom you came – your mother.
For without her he'd not have gone mad
and gone off with the gypsy.

BRAND: The hawk?—Gerd?

SHERIFF (*putting on hat*): Well, I must after my romany
runaway!
She's a mother too. Ah, we see Life!

Oh! (*Turning at door*) Happy Christmas?
And the same to the wife!

> *The* SHERIFF *goes out into the snow, slamming the door.*

> *The candle gutters, and throws weird shadows on the walls.*

BRAND (*slowly*): Gerd. My mother. My mother, through Gerd,
swung the scales of justice so I
chose; and condemned my own child to die?
The great scales which weigh all guilt
are grounded on the side of sin;
and the counterweight God seeks is us –
is our will to sacrifice.
That truth we overlay with lies,
for fear of knowing it. Sacrifice?

> (*Stopping by the candle*)

But by what sacrifice might I be
His blinding light, so the world might see
the pattern justifying the pain?
For so subtly woven in
is right with wrong and truth with lie,
that, in a world which could not see
the agony set against all time,
my sacrifice might seem to be
a crime, and a folly! (*Pacing restlessly*)
                                Oh, for some way
to be quite sure – quite sure –
– to pray?

> (*Halting*)

To pray for a sign? I cannot pray.
Yet – deep in sorrow – when the child slept
and would not wake with weeping and I wept
no more – did I not pray?
Was that not prayer which bore me then
beyond these shutters, beyond this room,
beyond this web which binds me down
to night, night! night! night!
Oh, Agnes, who sees beyond this dark –
Agnes, my eyes! – bring me light!

Suddenly the room is filled with the light of all the festival candles, which
AGNES *brings in on a tray.*

Ah! (BRAND *is startled into a cry*)

AGNES : Brand, what is it? What is it?

BRAND : The light. (*Fighting back to composure again*) The Christmas
candles.

AGNES : Yes. I've lighted them all. You told me to.

BRAND (*absently*) : The blinding light.

AGNES : Oh, I shouldn't have left you in the dark.

BRAND : No, no. It's all right.

AGNES : And how cold it has become in here! You must be
shivering.

BRAND : No, no. I'm all right. (*He turns away*)

AGNES (*talking more or less to herself as she goes to window*): See, this
candlestick shall stand . . . so! (*She draws the curtain*) The light
can spread out on to the snow and turn it into a gold quilt – his
covering. And he can see the warm glow through the glass.
Oh, but the window is veiled with tears. Wait, my lamb and
I'll wipe its face clear. Then the candle will smile at you. (*Wiping
the glass with her apron*)

BRAND (*to himself*): When will this sea of sorrow cease its restless
rocking? She must be freed of this fantasy. For, cradled in that
dream, she'll be rocked into madness by that sea. (*Softly*) Agnes.

AGNES : Now! There! It is clear. (*Standing back to look*) It's as if
the pane of glass had quite gone – as if to the room had been
added on a box bed, and the candle shone in, on his snowy
eiderdown. He sleeps. Sh! He's no longer cold.

BRAND : Oh, Agnes, this is not the way.

AGNES : Sh! Be quiet! (*Turning*) Oh! (*Flatly*) What did you say?

BRAND : You should not have drawn back these curtains again.

AGNES : It was only my dream – my fantasy.

BRAND: That fantasy can only lead to dreadful things. Draw them again.

AGNES (*imploringly*): Brand!

BRAND: Draw them. You must. Draw them close.

AGNES: Oh, don't be so harsh. It cannot be right!

BRAND: Draw them. Draw them!

AGNES *turns and draws the curtains and violently closes the shutters too.*

AGNES: There! (*Defiantly*) Oh! (*Bursting into tears*) How far will you drive me? I am so tired.

BRAND: We both must go all the way;
for our great sacrifice was in vain
if now we withhold one thing from *all*.

AGNES: I have given *all*. Ask more of me if you can. I have the courage of poverty. Ask! I have no cherished possessions now.

BRAND: You still possess and cherish this dream.

AGNES: Oh, uproot my heart too! Uproot my heart! For it is my torment! (*Shuddering*) Your way is too narrow – too steep for me.

BRAND: For the Will there is no other way.

AGNES: And what of the way of Mercy!

BRAND: It is paved with the stones of sacrifice.
First the Will, to pave the way
towards that mercy – towards that day
when His blinding light shall shine on you,
and you shall see God's face.

AGNES: *His* face!

     AGNES *stares ahead of her, trembling, almost trance-like.*

The words of the Bible – Brand!

BRAND: What words? What is it you see? (*Troubled*)

AGNES: 'Who sees the face of God shall *die*!' And I *will* . . .

BRAND (*quickly*): ... No! (*Throwing his arms about her*) You shall not see Him! Close your eyes!

AGNES: Close my eyes?

BRAND: These eyes. My sight! (*Slowly*) My sight. No.

AGNES: Oh, why do you torture yourself so?

BRAND: Because, by God's love, *I love you.*

AGNES (*she goes to him, and then looking up at his face*): Drive me; but never leave me.

BRAND: Never. (*He holds her as if in fear of losing her*)
Peace be with and around you and, through you,
come to me, on my way
– the narrow way. (*Releasing her*)
But now I must leave you for a little,
for I must plan the next step–
the great new church.

He moves to his study door.

AGNES: Brand, while you are working, may I
move the shutters a little?
They make me feel so shut in.
May I? Just ajar – a little way?

BRAND (*pitifully shaking his head*): No.

BRAND *goes into his room and closes the door. For a moment* AGNES *stands still.*

AGNES (*turning like a caged thing*):
My breast feels locked by a lock with no key.
I must get out! I must run away!
I feel this house suffocating me.
Run away? Wherever I'd go I'd see his eyes watching me. No.

She listens at BRAND'S *door.*

(*Turning from door*)

He toys with his dreams. Why may not I
be allowed to build *my* little temple too?
Shall I dare?

(*She goes carefully to the window*) Dare I open
the shutters? Dare I banish the night from his dark nursery?
No – the child is not there – a spirit – a soul
– at Christmas – the children's season! Sh! (*She listens*)
Oh, was that a child's cry?
Oh! If you are a spirit fly away!
Go where there is light and joy
and gay companions. Go south! Go south!
And don't say that your father shut you out:
for he made your wreath leaf by leaf,
– weeping. The snow will preserve that grief
out there in ice –
No! (*She makes as if to open
the shutters. Her hands fall by her side.*)

(*Her hands touch the linen chest*)

Oh! (*Almost recoiling from the chest. She
looks furtively at* BRAND'S *door*) But, surely God
would not grudge me my memories
at this time – the birth of his son?
(*With sudden decision*) I must see my treasures once again!
I must! I *will* see them.

Feverishly she raises the great lid and gets out the baby clothes one by one

The veil – the cloak – and the christening gown!

BRAND *comes out from his study, meaning to say something to* AGNES.
He stops still and remains standing, watching her.

BRAND (*aside*): Forever this fluttering over the grave. The same
games played in the garden of death.

AGNES (*continuing to herself*): His scarf – and the little blue coat! It
was so long and yet how soon he grew into it. Mittens! Shoes!
A lace cap and – the coat with the swansdown hood. The coat
he was wrapped in ready to go, on that awful night. When I laid
it away I was weary to the point of death.

BRAND (*aside*): Spare me this, Lord!
I cannot smash her last temple of dreams
with its precious idols. If it must be,
then send another to do it – not me!

AGNES (*rambling on unaware of him*):
  Tear-embroidered and crushed in sorrow
  – creased after tears – keeping the horror
  of that awful choice – (*voice rising*) sanctified
  to sacrifice. Not poor! I have lied.
  I am *rich* in these! I am ... (*Turning*) Ah! ...

AGNES *cries out as she sees* BRAND *standing watching her. At the same time there is a knocking on the door and it is thrown open to admit a* GYPSY WOMAN *with a child in her arms. She is in tatters and there is snow about her clothes.*

GYPSY : Ah, my dear, share these pretty clothes with me! – with a poor starved gypsy and her baby boy! Look at his rags! Look! See! Look, sir!

BRAND (*in an appalled voice*): Woman, come inside. Close the door.

AGNES (*afraid as the woman closes the door but stays by it*): What do you want here? Who has sent you?

GYPSY : The Sheriff and his gang are after us, like a pack of blood-hounds. If he finds us he'll lock us up again. If I can get something to wrap the baby in I'll get through the snow and get right away out of this district. But he's cold as death now. Will you give us some clothes?

BRAND : Agnes——(*As she hesitates*)

AGNES (*fearfully*): Yes?

BRAND : Is your duty not clear?

AGNES : Brand – not to such a woman – not to her!

BRAND : This woman and child have a right to them.

GYSPY : Come on. Give me your cast-offs. I'll take them all – silk dresses or rags.

BRAND : Agnes, choose.

AGNES : It is sacrilege!

BRAND : It is sacrifice.
  Our son died in vain if you withhold anything.

AGNES (*broken*): Then, let your will be done!
  I will tear up the roots of my heart.
  Here, woman, take your part
  of my dearest treasures.

GYSPY: That's it! (*Taking some*)

BRAND: Part?
  Agnes, – part?

AGNES: I would rather fall, struck down dead,
  than let them *all* be torn from me.
  She cannot *need* more.

BRAND: When you bought it all for him was *all* too much?

AGNES: Woman, come.
  Here, take my child's own christening gown –
  his dress – scarf, coat – yes, this coat!
  It is a good protection against the night wind.

(*Bitterly*)

Your child shall not die. It has a hood
with swansdown. Take it all!

BRAND: Is that all?

GYPSY: The chest's empty. Thank you, my dear! Thank you . . .
  sir!

The GYPSY *slips out of the door with the clothes.*

AGNES *stands as though going through some inner struggle.*

AGNES: Brand.

BRAND: Yes.

AGNES: Will anything more be asked of me?

BRAND: What you have now given away,
  was it given *willingly*?

AGNES: No.

BRAND : Then what you gave was thrown away;
and the demand still hangs over you.

(Moving to study door)

AGNES : Brand!

BRAND : Yes. What is it?

AGNES : I lied. I did not give her them all. *(With difficulty)* I kept
one thing.

> *From her breast she takes out a baby's lace cap.*

It holds the bitterest tears of my life.

BRAND : Then, remain subject to your fears and your cherished
possessions.

AGNES : No. *(With a great effort of will)*   Take her the cap too.
(Holding it out to him)

BRAND : Do you give it willingly?

AGNES *(tensely)*: Willingly.

BRAND *(taking the cap – himself in a sort of agony at the touch of it)*:
She may still be within call.

> BRAND *turns quickly and goes out of the main door.*

AGNES : Oh my heart! Yet gone are my fears.
Gone is all that tied me to earth. I am free!
The earth has no further use for me!

> BRAND *comes back in.*

I am free! Brand. I am free! Free!

BRAND : Agnes! *(Disturbed)*

AGNES *(Feverishly)*: Every one of my fears, unlocked from the
coffin of my breast, has tumbled down into the abyss, filling
the chasm across my path. I can cross! I can see – that beyond
this night is dawn – is light.

BRAND : Agnes! *(Troubled at her state)*

AGNES: You have freed my soul.
   The child *is* in Heaven! For the way of the Will
   there *is* victory!

BRAND: Victory? (*Staring at her*)

AGNES (*ecstatically*): Oh, look up to Heaven! There
   our son stands radiant by the throne,
   and stretches his arms to us down here!
   If I had a thousand mouths to cry,
   I would not call him back with one!
   There he lives and never dies.
   And God's face shines upon me!

His eyes! (*Crying out*)

BRAND *stands helplessly by.*

(*Turning to him*)

Oh, bless you for fighting my self for my soul.
I knew the agony of it all.
I saw you suffer for me.
But now we must part, and on you alone
falls the whole burden. Alone from now
you will face the full terror of this call
of *All* or *Nothing*.

BRAND: Alone? Why alone?

AGNES: Have you forgotten the Lord's own cry? –
   'Who sees my face shall surely *die*!'

BRAND (*as though struck*):
   What blinding light is this? No!
   No, never! I will not let you go!
   These hands shall hold you. Let who dares try!
   Agnes, I *will* not let you die!
   Let the earth lose motion – Take away light!
   But not *you*! Oh, not you, my sight!

AGNES: Would you quench this light in me –
   bind me and drop me back in the sea
   of sorrow's twisting tidal night?

BRAND: Oh, if far from here in some southern land
I could keep both life *and* light in you.

AGNES: No. Choose, Brand. Choose!

BRAND (*in great dread*): I have no choice.

AGNES: I am glad. (*Embracing him*)
You have faithfully guided one weary soul
forth from the mists. Watch by my bed,
till I fall asleep.

BRAND: Yes, *your* work is done.

AGNES (*as she goes*): Day over – and the candles lit.

(*As she takes the main candlestick*)

BRAND: Oh, Agnes——

AGNES: How I long to fall asleep.

AGNES *goes, carrying with her the branched candlestick and with it most of the light.*

BRAND (*clenching his hands against his breast*):
What is lost to God is gain.
Soul, stand firm! To the end, my soul!
For the victory is to lose *all*!

CURTAIN

ACT III

Scene 1

Some months later – late Spring. A bright morning.
Outside the New Church – which is fantastically grand for such a place.

Its door and the steps to it are within the scene.

Opposite the Church are rocks, and a steep slope, leading towards the uplands.

In preparation for the consecration of the new building, the SCHOOL-MASTER and the SEXTON are hanging festival decorations outside the entrance to the Church. They may well be a little the better for a festive nip.

SEXTON: There's none too much time, Schoolmaster.
This is to keep the procession in place.

He is hanging a leaf-garland from pole to pole in front of the Church steps.

SCHOOLMASTER: It's a regular Festival! (*Pointing off*)
The Fjord is almost white with sails.

SEXTON: Ah! In the old pastor's day
you'd never have had such a to-do.
Changing the shepherd has changed the sheep.
Then we lay like a flock asleep;
but now there's such life! – and trouble too!
I don't know which is better. Do you?

SCHOOLMASTER: Life! Sexton, Life!

SEXTON: With Pastor in the thick of it too?

SCHOOLMASTER: His superiors don't approve of it. Eh?
Oh, but Pastor's no fool.
He builds this new church; because what you need –
when everybody's disagreed
and people in an ugly mood,
is to institute some public scheme.
It can be any madman's dream –

67

like this – this 'Ice Church' built of wood –
But there's nothing so serves for distraction
as a bit of 'public action'. (*With a knowing nudge*)
And what I say is . . .

SEXTON (*interrupting*): . . . Ssh!

SCHOOLMASTER: What is it?

SEXTON: Hold your peace, Schoolmaster!

> *The organ is heard playing in the Church.*

(*Turning to the Schoolmaster*) Well?

SCHOOLMASTER: It's someone playing the organ.

SEXTON: It is *he*.

SCHOOLMASTER: What? Pastor?

SEXTON: Pastor.

SCHOOLMASTER: Pastor? Well!
He must have been up and about early.

SEXTON (*slyly*): I don't think the pillow of the pastoral bed
was crumpled at all by the pastoral head,
this last night.

SCHOOLMASTER: Really?

SEXTON: Things are not right with that poor man.
A secret sorrow has gnawed at him
ever since his poor wife died.
It's a sorrow he tries bravely to hide
but here and there it breaks out – so . . .

> *They listen and the organ music plays on.*

It's as if his heart did overflow.

SCHOOLMASTER: As if he talked to her, though she'd died.

SEXTON: As if one comforted, one cried.

> (*Wiping away a sentimental tear*)

SCHOOLMASTER: Yes – if only at every hour of the day
  one wasn't always obliged to defend
  one's dignity as a servant of State,
  one might weep. (*Blowing his nose*)

SEXTON: Yes.

> *Both looking to see that they are not observed.*

SCHOOLMASTER: Shall we, Sexton, dare to deal
  the death-blow to dignity – and just *feel*?

> *Looking at each other.*

SEXTON (*winking*): Schoolmaster... Where no one can see,
  there can't be anything to conceal.
  We are alone ... Let us just – *feel*!

They listen – losing themselves in the music. There is a sudden agonised discord on the organ; and silence. They look at each other in fright, then apprehensively at the Church door, which begins to open.

SCHOOLMASTER: The schoolchildren will be expecting me.
  (*Goes*)

SEXTON: I expect someone's expecting me too. (*Goes*)

Slowly the Church door swings open and BRAND *comes out. His black hair is grey. He seems taller. His face is strained.*

BRAND: There comes a point where the organ too
  shrieks out its insufficiency.
  For, in my world there seems no art,
  by which to express my full heart
  to God.
  (*Looking up at his new Church*)
  Great should His house be. That was the dream –
  that carried me through those months of pain
  and desolation. Great? Is it so?
  Is this the temple of my dreams?
  It this the cathedral whose great arch
  would, like a rainbow in the sky,
  span the earth and embrace the cry
  of a suffering world?

F

Or is it just fantasy
born of grief?

(*Turning from the church*)

Had Agnes lived I would be sure –
she in whose unclouded eye
Earth and Heaven were but the one tree
seen as the trunk and the greenery.

He notices the greenery of the festival decorations.

Wreaths and banners hung for *me*?
My name raised in gold letters there?
Children practising *my* praise?
I who now cannot pray!
God, give me back the power of prayer
or shut me in some animal's lair
where there's no light, no choirs sing,
and the evil is in remembering
this life!

The SHERIFF *comes in, in full, splendid – almost comic – uniform.*

SHERIFF: At last! (*Approaching*) At last! The great day!
Congratulations, Brand, my friend.
I brought the ceremonial key – for the door.
(*Aside*) Is he listening to me?
(*To* BRAND) You'll test it in the lock before . . . ?

BRAND (*interrupting*): Yes, yes! Yes, Sheriff. (*Flatly, as he turns*)
Must you wear these clothes?

SHERIFF: Well, it's customary – The traditional dress.
All's set for success! Look at the crowd! (*Pointing off*)
People have been pouring in all day
from all parts of the district and now
the Dean himself has just arrived.
He's up at the house looking for you.

BRAND: The Dean – looking for me?

SHERIFF (*rubbing his hands*): Ah! the world's at your feet! How
does it feel? Eh? How does it feel?

BRAND: As though an icy band of steel
   gripped round my throat.

SHERIFF: Tut-tut!
   We'll have to get rid of that!
   You'll have to be full-throated now,
   if you're going to fill that church with your voice.

(*Looking up at it*)

   Mag-ni-fi-cent edifice!

BRAND: You think so?

SHERIFF: Think?

BRAND: That my church is great.

SHERIFF: *Think*? I know it is!

BRAND: It is?
   Great? Really great, you think——?

SHERIFF: Death and Destruction, man! It is great!
   Too great, in fact, for folk like these.

SHERIFF (*pointing off*): Look at them now – like a swarm of bees –
   astir, yet hushed, and ready to rise
   when you give the word for all to praise
   our new church. Ah! It's amazing size
   has silenced all the cries they raised
   when the old ruin was brought low. Eh?

BRAND: Yes, I see it now.

SHERIFF: See what?

BRAND: That we have merely shifted the people's view
   from an old ruin to this great, new, . . . 'edifice'.
   And yet, it is *small*.
   And they must be made to see it as small.

SHERIFF: Come, man! The people are satisfied.
   Why, if it was the size of a herring crate,
   who cares – so long as they think it's great?

Dammit! It's a holiday; *and*, for your own sake
I'd advise you to soft-pedal all this talk
of it being *small*.

BRAND: For my sake? Why?

SHERIFF: Well!
– the Parish Council, in the first place,
have subscribed to give you a silver chalice –
the inscription on which would look rather absurd
if you try to substitute the word
'small' for 'great'. And my speech!
My speech! wouldn't apply at all! –
if this mag-ni-fi-cent edifice – were *small*.
No, Brand, it's worth some compromise.
Use a bit of tact. Do you happen to know
why the Dean himself has honoured us?

BRAND: No.

SHERIFF (*confidentially*): Because the King may honour *you* –
with Cross of the Order. There!

BRAND (*turning away*): My honour is a cross I wear
for all occasions – from another King.

SHERIFF: Honestly! – You'd drive a saint mad!
But for your own sake . . .

BRAND (*turning in exasperation*): . . . Stop!
All this talk is waste of breath.
I haven't meant greatness which any fool
could measure with a three-foot rule;
but that which hidden still radiates light;
though chill, yet sets afire the soul;
which spans life like star-studded night,
which – which – Oh! Leave me! I'm worn out!
Argue, explain, talk if you will –
but not to me.

BRAND *turns away towards the Church.*

SHERIFF (*to self*):
    Greatness, 'like star-studded night,'
    'hidden, yet radiating light' . . . ?
    Ever since his poor wife died . . .
    Ah yes! there he goes again –
    looking at the graves. It must be the strain.
    Good Lord! Here comes the Dean!
    And I haven't yet put on my chain.
    I'm half dressed!

The SHERIFF *goes quickly.*

BRAND: Agnes, this empty game wearies me so.
    No one wins; one dares not give way,
    and the lonely fighter becomes his own foe.

The DEAN *comes in. He is obviously the town-bred dignitary. But his formal dignity contrasts unfavourably with* BRAND'S *natural dignity.*

DEAN (*at a little distance*): Ah! Brand. There you are!

BRAND (*turning – resignedly*): Yes, Dean.

DEAN: I came to 'spy out the land'.
    I see you have the key.
    And that's the great door. (*Turning to him*) Brand my son,
    until this time you have fought alone
    in this fjord, like a christian knight
    in dark lands. But to-day – to-day –
    I bring the power of Church *and* State
    to support you in your great fight.
    My dear boy, you look pale and ill!

BRAND: It is not my own strength which will win the day.

DEAN: No. But never fear! Never fear!
    It will all run through without a hitch.
    And the work! This mag-ni-fi-cent edifice!
    It is the topic of every tongue –
    every tongue! And the luncheon! –
    What a mag-ni-fi-cent spread!
    I have just come from the parsonage . . .
    But no more of that, for the moment – er –
    It was another matter really brought me here.

(With a change of tone, taking him by the arm)

There is one simple little point,
which, henceforth, I am sure you will see
is put to rights. You may know what I mean.
It concerns your *official* duties, as such.
Heretofore you have laid much too much
emphasis in your pastoral plan
on the *individual* needs of man.
Good Lord! Don't think I'm scolding you!
For here you have built this church, in a sense
out of your own pocket. But from this day hence
we are prepared to back your crusade.
Which brings up the matter of public expense.
You see all these State grants are not made
in blind charity, which might be in aid
of people and priests who could agitate
beliefs obnoxious to The State.
No. The State is no fool and its aim must be
to culture a state christianity;
for it sees – grant it that common sense –
that 'Good Christians' means 'Good Citizens!'
But it must have the ear of the priest on the spot;
who is after all – in his social role –
The State's official – is he not?

BRAND: I see – My soul must be bought,
before my church is subsidised.

DEAN: Come! You exaggerate my friend!
You are not committed to anything *wrong*.
Your faith in men's souls need not be less strong,
simply because at the same time
you serve the State.
But I hope I am making myself clear.

BRAND: Too clear. I am afraid
that I do not fit into the pigeon hole,
which the State provides for the standard soul.

DEAN: Oh indeed but you do. I mean – my friend *(confidentially)*
I understand that they intend

you for one on the very top shelf.
You are to rise.

BRAND (*wearily*): Aye – via the mud.

DEAN (*annoyed*): He who abases himself shall be raised up!

BRAND: Abases? *Degrades*, you mean.

DEAN: How could you say such a thing?
(*Angry*) Perhaps you do not realise
that I am merely assisting you to rise
by leaving the same door ajar
through which I rose to be——

BRAND (*cutting him short*): —— *what you are!*
(*Slowly*) Can you not see what you ask of me?
To renounce, when the Cock of State should crow,
all the ideals I stand for now?

DEAN: 'Renounce!' My friend, did I say such a thing?
No. I merely pointed out to you
what is in fact your official duty! (*Pause*)
Brand . . . if you'd rise out of this northern abyss,
it would befit you, my son, to see in the State
the framework on which you *may* grow great –
and you may——

BRAND: Oh! (*To self*) Let me break out of here!

DEAN: But – for those who'd rise to-day
the State *is* the stairway. Well! – that's that.
Don't be cast down. But do meditate
on what I have said. I must go.
When I preach I shall try to throw
my voice much higher to suit this great church.
My sermon will be on the abiding theme
of the smearing of the image of God –
with special reference to the chaos come now
into our troubled temporal scheme
of World Affairs. But first – I think –
I might do worse than have something to drink.
Till the ceremony! Tasteful decorations!

(Touching the garlands as he goes)

BRAND *(releasing a long sigh of pent-up feeling)*:
Ah! ! !
How right he is about the State
and how wrong about the state of man.
(He again turns towards AGNES' *grave)*
Agnes, they shall not drag me down,
with their high honours. I will go on –
alone. Alone? How can a man know
what he is, – alone? Oh!
If I could only meet just *one* kindred soul,
One who'd confirm what I hold here;
then might fear finally go.

(His eye catches something)

Who is that poor devil on the road – No! *(Incredulously)* Can it
be? – Einar. How strange! Einar!

EINAR *comes in.*

EINAR : That is my name.

EINAR *is pale, emaciated and in clerical black.*

BRAND : Oh, let me clap you to my heart. Here was I longing for
an old friend like you: a man with a heart not made of stone
and——*(as* EINAR *repels him)*

EINAR : Stand away!

BRAND *(amazed at his appearance)*: Are you all right? You look ill.

EINAR : I *have* been ill. *(Looking at* BRAND *defensively)*

BRAND : You still bear me a grudge for what happened, eh?

EINAR : No, You were not to blame at all.
You were merely the blind instrument
sent by Our Lord to save my soul.

BRAND *(considerably taken aback)*: What talk is this? – From you?

EINAR (*with fanatical intensity*): The language which *the saved* must speak, coming out of the night of Sin, is not of this world.

BRAND (*amazed*): 'Sin!' 'Saved?' I heard you had struck a very different path.

EINAR: I *had*, in my pride, when my paintings seemed great. But all my gifts were as nought – till the Lord's hand had humbled me.

BRAND: Humbled you?

EINAR: Gambling – Drink. For months I lay in hospital – a broken man. They almost brought me back from the dead.

BRAND: Indeed? And now?

EINAR: I am going as a missionary. To Africa. I sail from here.

BRAND: Won't you stay at all?

EINAR: Thank you, no.

BRAND: And doesn't any memory from the past prompt you to ask about . . .

EINAR: About what?

BRAND: About one who would be so sorry to see this sad difference in you now.

EINAR: Oh – that girl. That was all in the days before the Blood of the Lamb had washed me clean.

BRAND: I'd like you to know, she became my wife.

EINAR: To our Faith, such things are not *fundamental*.

BRAND: No? Well, our life together was rich in both joy and sorrow; our little boy died.

EINAR : Nor is that *fundamental*, either.

BRAND : No?
But indeed his dear soul was more of a loan,
than a gift from God. And the day will dawn
when we'll meet again. But, afterwards, she, –
she herself was taken away.
Over there the grass is green on their graves.

EINAR : Neither is that *fundamental*.

BRAND : No?

EINAR : It doesn't concern The Faithful. What we must know
is not *where* or even why she died, but *how*?

BRAND (*gently*) : She blessed God for all this life gave,
even as He took it away.

EINAR : Yes, yes, but how was her Faith?

BRAND (*with great pride*) : Immovable.

EINAR : In whom?

BRAND : Why, in God.

EINAR : Only in God? Then she was not *saved*? Alas!
Doomed!

BRAND (*amazed*) : What did you say?

EINAR : Without *Salvation* she is doomed. Without the Lamb——

BRAND (*with cold fury*) : Get you gone!

EINAR *retreats from* BRAND'S *anger.*

EINAR (*excitedly*) : The Lord of Hell will have you too.
The Devil will set his claws on you,
so you will die eternally,–
like her!

BRAND : Like her!
You snivelling wretch! Do *you* dare condemn *her*?

EINAR : I am saved!

BRAND (*advancing on him*): Damn your smug soul!

EINAR (*retreating*): Damnation is yours! I see the horn
of Satan on your forehead now! I am saved!
(*Going*) But *you* shall burn!

EINAR goes.

(*Off*) You shall burn!

BRAND stands, shocked; watching him go.

BRAND: So that's the other side of your bright coin – Frivolity!
(*He turns*) Now all the chains are snapped.
Now, I go forward from this hour
to unmapped heights in country where
perhaps no man dares follow me.
Alone? Alone, if it must be.
Alone.

The sound of the crowd off is heard.

The SHERIFF hurries in.

SHERIFF: Pastor, old man, you must get a move on!
The procession is formed up ready to march. Come.

BRAND: Let them march.

SHERIFF: Without you?
The whole parish is up at the parsonage
shouting for the Pastor. I hear them now.
I have kept a lane through the crowd for you.

BRAND: I will wait here.

SHERIFF: Are you mad?
Come! If the crowd push in as they're doing now
there soon won't be any way back.

Sound of hubbub off.

Good Lord! Look! Here they come! –
carrying the whole clergy before them!
The procession's ruined! For goodness sake!
Pastor use your authority.

They'll frisk the fence – They have! It's too late!
They are all over everywhere now!

The CROWD *breaks in, in complete disorder, carrying bits of the procession with it. The* SCHOOLMASTER *is in the fore.*

CROWD (*calling*): Pastor Priest! Priest!

SCHOOLMASTER (*pointing to the church steps where he stands*):
There he is!

SEXTON: Give the opening signal now!

The DEAN *struggles to the fore.*

DEAN: Sheriff! Control them!

CROWD: Pastor! Pastor! Speak to us! Speak!

General hubbub of crowd.

BRAND *holds up his hand for silence.*

FISHERMAN: Can't you see he's holding up his hand? Silence!

CROWD: Quiet! Silence now!

Silence is achieved.

BRAND (*with quiet intensity*):
   You have come, my people, to that place
   where you must make a choice of path.
   Here, in you eager eyes I see
   that great church shine which, by your will,
   we yet may build. There, behind me,
   stands this puny church: and *you*
   must choose the greater of the two.

SEXTON: The parson's possessed!

FISHERMAN: He's mad!

WOMAN: Mad?

BRAND: No! I *was* mad!
   I was mad to think that in this church
   I might imitate for you

Life's infinite grandeur. I was mad
to think that this ugly construction might be
my gift to God. But now I see
that what the Lord requires of us
is not some empty gift like this,
but *All* or *Nothing* – no gift less
than *all* of our life!
And to the subtle fiend who cries,
'Compromise! Compromise!'
we must answer, 'All! All!'

CROWD (*amazed*) : All ? All ?

SCHOOLMASTER : 　　　　　Lead us, Brand!
With you we *will* risk all!

DEAN : We have come to open this church!

SHERIFF : Open the church!

BRAND : Which church? This church? (*Pointing to building*)

WOMAN : Your church!

BRAND : But is this the temple of my dreams?
Is this the church which I had seen
to shelter you not only at prayer,
but cover your broad backs bent in work,
your old by the fire, your young in the dark? –
to shelter all within whose breast
lies that sweet and divine unrest
of being God's creature? It was to be so
that each and every joy of life
should congregate beneath one roof! –
from the cataract up there in the snow,
to the foaming river there below,
to the storm-sob whispering over the sea –
that all those through faith *should* here infuse
Man with Nature, and in God's house
the organ peal and the voices cry,
like Adam's praise upon The First Day!

FISHERMAN : Lead us! whichever way you say!

SCHOOLMASTER : Lead us! We can do all things with you !

CROWD: All! All!

DEAN: My flock! (*Getting above crowd*)

CROWD: The Dean!
The Dean! Sh! Sh! The Dean!

DEAN: You must not listen to this man!
His is not the faith of a Christian at all!

BRAND: No!
For my faith requires a soul!
And point out a so-called Christian here
who has not thrown his soul away
in sipping a cup he dared not drain,
and yet who, when the cup is dry,
will creep as a cripple to God's feet –
and whine for mercy! What a defeat! –
for One who said that the Kingdom's gate
would swing wide open to the child
with all his wild vitality! Come!

                    (*Turning to crowd again*)

Come – you who have the will –
and build His church! You who still
have a child's vision and a child's joy!
Come!

SHERIFF: Unlock the church door!

BRAND: No!
The church I speak of has no door.
The sky is its roof; the earth its floor!
And all Nature is hers! All!

CROWD: All!

The CROWD *begins to surge about the steps.*

                    All!!
                         All! The Day!
                                    Away! All!

BRAND *now that the crowd is won has turned to the door.*

WOMAN: It will be! It will be!

FISHERMAN: Life and worship the one thing!

CROWD: The one thing! All! The day!

DEAN (*shouting*): Sheriff, he's opening the door!

SHERIFF: No! He's locking it!

CROWD: All!
                    The Day!

SHERIFF: Look!

DEAN: The key! The ceremonial key!

> BRAND *holds up his hand and in it is the great key.*

CROWD: Look! The key!

> *The crowd is hushed.*

BRAND: Here I am no longer priest!
I take back this church – my mistaken gift.
And no one else shall have its key!

> *He hurls the key out into the fjord.*

> *The* CROWD *gasps.*

DEAN: Into the fjord! The ceremonial key!
It's desecration!

CROWD: All! Lead us! All!

> BRAND *strides into the crowd.*

SHERIFF (*getting up where* BRAND *has been and shouting*):
I will charge you all with a breach of the peace!

BRAND: It is a peace that should be broken!

CROWD: Lead on, Brand!

BRAND (*moving through crowd*): Come with me! –
to that church whose night ceiling will be
the track of stars and, in the day,
clouds or the limits to all sight!

CROWD: The path! The path! Lead the way!

BRAND *reappears above the crowd on the slope that leads to the uplands.*

BRAND: Throughout this country we shall go,
uprooting every snare which now
holds the people's spirit down
in dread of Death and The Grave!
We shall lift up! Oh, we shall save!
But where there stands in our way –
Fear! Frivolity! Fantasy!
we shall without mercy destroy!
And *then*, on the day of victory,
all the people's hidden joy
will burst from their hearts and God regain
the spirit he had lodged with men!
Towards that day, come! Come all!

BRAND *goes up slope with the* CROWD *following.*

CROWD(*going*):   All!
                        All!
                              All! Away!

SHERIFF (*calling after them*): You are all going to your doom up
there among the ice and snow! Think what you're doing! Stop
and think!

FISHERMAN: The Voice of Compromise!

CROWD (*off and mounting*): All! All! All! All!

The SHERIFF *and the* DEAN *are left alone.*

DEAN: Oh! (*Almost in tears*) Stripped of my whole flock!

SHERIFF: Come! Cheer up, Dean. He will end up in disgrace.
The victory will be ours in the end.

DEAN: Victory? (*Ready to weep*) With not one sheep left in the fold?

SHERIFF: Have no fear. There's no call to weep – (*Slyly*) Not if
I know your sheep.

Sound of CROWD *fading away.*

Come.

The SHERIFF *goes off purposively.*

The DEAN *follows in perplexity.*

CURTAIN

SCENE 2

Later the same day.

The precipitous path above the fjord. (The same as Act I. – when BRAND *looked down on his home)*
There is snow among the rocks, but it is the misty weather of The Thaw.

BRAND *climbs into view and looks back down.*

BRAND: Up here! This way!

VOICE (*off below*): It will soon be dark.

VOICE (*off below*): It's too steep!

BRAND: The steep way is the shortest way!

The SCHOOLMASTER *comes into view.*

SCHOOLMASTER: Brand, the Ice Church is up there. It's no time of the year to go near that! Listen. The ice melts thin at The Thaw, and the whole massive roof of snow rests on such a delicate shell that one thrown stone might bring it down in an avalanche. It would sweep us all into the fjord.

As BRAND *pauses for breath, the* SEXTON *climbs into view.*

SEXTON: The crowd won't follow on, Pastor.

BRAND: Why?

SEXTON: They're exhausted.

SCHOOLMASTER: They badly need food and drink.

Some of the CROWD *come into view.*

G

VOICES OF CROWD: How long must we struggle on?
When is it likely to last till?
What will we get out of it all?

SCHOOLMASTER: Yes. It wasn't very clearly explained, you
know when we were down there, Pastor.

BRAND: Then it shall be made clear now. (*Turning to address the
crowd below*) How long will this struggle last? Until the day we
die!

CROWD: Die!!! ?

BRAND: Until we have battled to the end, and our every fibre has
answered the cry of *All* or *Nothing*.

WOMAN (*horrified*): Until we die?

SEXTON: You promised us *victory*! – not sacrifice!

BRAND: And I promise you victory still! But to fall in the front
ranks of a new world is to live forever. Come!

WOMAN: He's leading us to our deaths – not victory!

CROWD: He wants to kill us!

SEXTON: Let's turn back. It's dangerous up here.

FISHERMAN: No, not now! We can't go back now.

SCHOOLMASTER: But we daren't go up into the snow. It is
dangerous up by the Ice Church. There are avalanches. Let's go
back. Oh! Look!

MAN: The Dean! On a hill pony! Climbing up after us. Oh!

There is a movement in those of the crowd visible, and the DEAN *pants
into view with a riding whip in his hand.*

DEAN (*breathlessly*): Oh! my poor sheep! What are you doing up
here, amid the mists and the snow?
Not only are your souls in danger now
– but your lives!

WOMAN (*Ingratiatingly*): Don't be hard on us, sir.
We *want* to go home.

BRAND: Choose again! Choose your way!

SHERIFF (*off*): Hullo! Hullo!

The SHERIFF *climbs up, puffing and red in the face.*

SHERIFF: Ha! Lucky for you I have found you! Down below a new day is dawning for our little parish!

SEXTON: A new day? How?

SHERIFF: The Fjord is boiling.

SCHOOLMASTER: Boiling?

SHERIFF: With fish!

WOMAN: Fish!

SHERIFF: A shoal!

CROWD: A shoal of fish!

CROWD: Fish! Fish! (*The word is passed from mouth to mouth in a ripple of excitement*)

BRAND: Choose, cravens, between the call of God, and the croak of this raven!

SHERIFF: Oh don't heed *me*! Only, it might be as well to follow your own common sense, that's all.

DEAN (*suddenly*): It is a miracle! This shoal of fishes was sent to you to show how you have gone astray! A finger from heaven points the way! Back down to the fjord!

BRAND: If you listen to him, you are doomed!

WOMAN: A shoal of fishes! Food!

DEAN: And prosperity!

SHERIFF: And what *is* this mad crusade anyway?

SEXTON: The Pastor, he's mad.

SHERIFF: No. He's just a fanatic. They never mean what they say.

FISHERMAN: He *did* lie to us. Well – I mean to say——

WOMAN: He deceived us about the victory.

DEAN: He is a simple uncultured man carried away.

SHERIFF: A downright bad character – that's what he is.

DEAN: He let his poor mother pass away, without the sacrament.

FISHERMAN: That is true!

SHERIFF: You might say that he killed his own child.

CROWD: It's true!

WOMAN: *And* killed his wife with hardship too!

DEAN: Bad son, bad father, bad husband! Now! Could there be a worse Christian?

CROWD: No!

BRAND: Oh! I see the mark upon the brow of this generation. I see where you'll go!

MAN: Drive him to-Hell-out-of-it! Go on! Get away!

FISHERMAN: Drive him up into the snow!

> *He throws a stone at* BRAND. *Others follow suit.*

CROWD: Drive him away! Stone him!

> BRAND *is hit, and goes, blindly retreating from the stones.*

DEAN: My children! Children!

SHERIFF (*roaring*): Stop! I tell you! Stop, you fools!

> CROWD *stops shouting and throwing stones.*

You idiots! Do you want to be buried in an avalanche!

DEAN: Oh! My children!——

> CROWD *becomes quiet.*

Shedding blood is not Christian! The call of the Church must always be *Caritas*! Charity! Now—— Let us go from this dangerous place.

SHERIFF: Back to the fjord and the fish! Down with you!

CROWD: The fish! The fish! Down! Home! The fish!

DEAN (*almost tearful*): The Lord will forgive you all! Go down!

SEXTON (*going*): Now there's real Christian charity!

SCHOOLMASTER (*going*): Yes, feeling; without vulgarity!

The SCHOOLMASTER *and* SEXTON *go after the* CROWD.

DEAN: Well—— (*With a weary smile*) All this will weld them into one faction. Thank the Lord for – 'reaction'? eh?

SHERIFF: Thank *me*.

DEAN (*surprised*): Thank *you*, Sheriff? We owe it to a near miracle. The shoal of fish.

SHERIFF: That was not strictly true.

DEAN: You mean there was not a shoal?

SHERIFF: Well, do you blame me? – in such an *emergency*?

DEAN: Not in such an *emergency*. But ——

SHERIFF: See! There he goes stumbling up in the snow – The lone soldier now!
Poor old Brand! It is hard too,
that *all* the people should turn on him.

DEAN: True! True! (*Turning to go*) But——
'Vox populi vox dei'. After you!

The DEAN *and* SHERIFF *go off, down towards the fjord.*

The wind whistles in the rocks.

Slowly BRAND *returns. The setting sun is on him. He is badly cut about the face and hands. He looks off after the descending crowd.*

BRAND:
And not one crawled clear of the abyss.
Out of all those, not one – not *one*!

He sinks wearily on to a rock.

So ends my day.
My childhood was one long nightmare,
through which I struggled towards this day
when in manhood I would rise

to strip the morning to its skies,
and scour God's image clean of all stain.
I'd tear apart the shutters of home –
for night was not real, and light would come
streaming from the world outside.
But now I find night over all –
night behind night, wall behind wall
of this impenetrable dark.
And the one way out – the one way through
by which to pierce the crust of night
and let God's light stream on Man's eyes –
the *only* means, is a sacrifice
beyond the comprehension of Man.
And so he'll die. He will not rise.
And the world will wither.

Suddenly rising and pointing as the wind whistles around the rocks.

See now! Hell-for-leather bent,
those three witches whom I had sent
to stark perdition! Ride your wild wind!
The world's you open course! Ride on,
Fear! - Frivolity! - Fantasy!

Drunk with exhaustion. He sways on his feet.

Not for us the cup – drained;
not for us the thorns – red;
not for us the figure strained
across The Cross. We are the dead –
who cannot see and dare not feel
His gasp against the Roman steel.
His wounds may cry: we hear no call;
for His cry is too great, and we are so small –
Oh! Age of the human pygmy freak,
who cannot hear his own soul shriek!

He falls forward in the snow: and lies as though in a faint.

The storm wind rises. Music is heard.

Slowly he raises his head and looks fearfully around.

Have I dreamed all this up till now?
Were mine the illusions of a sick mind?

Is He gone? He who designed
man in His image? Our Creator – has he
lost control of His earth? And do we
go on without Him from to-day?
Am I my own God? I . . . He?

A VOICE (*chanting through the soughing wind, and the music*):
> Never, never shall you be
> like Him. He was Divinity.
> Creature of the flesh you'll stay.
> Turning or keeping to His Way,
> you are lost, lost, lost!

BRAND (*softly*):
'Creature of the flesh you'll stay –
lost, lost, lost! Lost!'
I must believe it. Unhappy me!

A VOICE:
> Worm, you cannot be like Him!
> You have suckled death. Choose!
> Against or with Him you will still lose.
> For you were created for earthly life;
> and He is no richer for your strife.

BRAND (*turning – his eye catching something in the mists*):
Am I mad? Is this madness?
I am seeing things I cannot see,
Agnes – my eyes, come back to me!
I am no longer the knight who'd slay
the dragon Despair. I am desperate now –
cold, sick and alone in the dark.
Ah! . . . Agnes! (*Crying out*)

In a clear patch of the mist THE FIGURE OF AGNES *appears.*

THE FIGURE OF AGNES:
No, you are not dreaming, Brand.
But you did dream everything up till now.
It was a lie.

BRAND: My life a lie?
I *am* mad!

AGNES : No!
But, Brand, it is true that you are still
confused by those nightmares which made you ill.
I have the cure.

BRAND (*eagerly*) : Oh! Give it me!

AGNES : All these awful delusions have come
from three simple words.

BRAND (*apprehensively*) : Three words?

AGNES : These you must *will* to erase from your brain;
and the madness will pass like the mist and the rain.

BRAND (*fearfully*) : Three words?
Speak them. Speak them.

AGNES : *All or nothing.*

BRAND : No!——(*Crying out*)
It cannot be true!

AGNES : It is!

BRAND : God help me! The hawk is up again,
and hovers over our bare heads.

AGNES : Be kind; be tolerant, and come with me!

BRAND : No!

Turning back towards the fjord.

AGNES (*crying out*) : Stop! You are on the edge of an abyss!
Brand, what would you do?

BRAND (*with an effort of will*) : What I must:—
Live that struggle, which till now
has been only dream – only fantasy!

AGNES : Would you now, freely and awake,
take that same nightmare ride again?

BRAND : Free and awake.

AGNES : Sacrifice the child?

BRAND : Sacrifice the child.

AGNES : Brand!

BRAND : I must!

AGNES : And trapping me in the sunless air,
    kill me with burdens I could not bear?

BRAND : I must. I must. *I will!*

AGNES (*as he again makes to go*) :
    Are you not forgetting there was a reward –
    the raising of the people up?
    And have they not refused your word,
    betrayed you, beaten, and cast you out?

BRAND : I do not suffer for my own gain.
    I do not fight for *my* victory.
    I fight for Paradise for Man
    on God's Earth!

AGNES : But Sin! Sin!
    You cannot cross the moat of Sin
    towards Eden!

BRAND : I can! I can!
    (*With rising voice*) For the Lord has left
    one way in:—
    through the yearning heart of a man!

THE FIGURE *goes.*

THE VOICE OF THE FIGURE (*calling out*) : Die!!!...
    There is no further use for you
    upon this earth.

BRAND : Ah! See now!
    It beats up and away, like a great hawk.
    That was not my Agnes. No.
    That was the Spirit of Compromise.

GERD *comes in. She carries a rifle.*

GERD : Did you see the hawk? (*Eagerly*) Did you see the hawk?

BRAND : Yes, girl, this time I *did* see it.

GERD : Which way did it go ? Quick!
Tell me! We'll after him, and finish him off.
I've got the reindeer-hunter's gun.

BRAND : Nothing I know of will kill that bird.
It will come again in some other form.

GERD : I could kill it if I could get near.
I'm not so mad as folk say.
I can hit the mark.

BRAND (*turning wearily to go*): It may be so, child.
It may be so.

GERD : Priest, you're lame.
Oh – what's happened to you ?

BRAND : I was hunted – by the people.

GERD (*peering at him*): And there's blood on your brow.

BRAND : They stoned me – the people.

GERD : You used to speak with a song in your voice;
but just listen to you now
– like dry leaves rustling before the snow.

BRAND (*to self*): Yes – All of them, child –
betrayed me.

GERD : Oh! . . . (*Looking at him wide-eyed*)
Now I see who you really are!
I took you for a priest! Bah!
What do I care for the priest and his crew!
But you – you are the Greatest of Men!

BRAND : To my shame I almost thought so.

GERD : Please, may I look at your hands ?

BRAND : My hands ? (*As she takes them*)

GERD : Ah!
The print of the nails!

BRAND (*recoiling*): The print of the nails!

GERD : You're the man on the crucifixion tree!

BRAND: Stand away from me! Get away from me!

GERD: No. I want to fall at your feet.

BRAND: Go! Child!

GERD (*excitedly*): Blood!
  The blood to save us all—— Look,
  is going to waste, staining the snow!

BRAND (*appalled*): My blood?
  I, who do not have the power
  to save my own soul!

GERD (*getting stone*): Take this big stone.
  Roll it. Roll it down on top of them.
  It will start an avalanche which might fill
  the whole fjord and kill! Kill! Kill!

BRAND (*shaking his head*): No!
  A man must strive until the end.

GERD: But not *you*! You are the Leader. The One,
  who brought the mark of the nails through death.

BRAND: I am the most utterly abject worm
  that ever crawled on the face of the earth.

  Some light comes through the mist; and GERD *looks up.*

GERD: Do you know where you are standing now?

BRAND (*absently*):
  On the first step of a long, long ascent;
  and Oh!—— so footweary!

GERD (*with childish petulance*): Answer me!
  Do you know where you are standing now?

BRAND (*absently*): Not till this mist clears away.

GERD: But it *is* clearing. And, Look! The Ice Church!

  (*Pointing up*)

Towering above us – up into the sky!

BRAND: The Ice Church!

Both look up with the red sunset on them.

GERD: The sun is staining the ice red!
And on every pinnacle I see grow
thorns of ice! But they are melting. Oh!

BRAND: Like drops of blood. (*To self*)

GERD: We may still go to church, come.
There is the Ice Church door – with the pillars of snow!

BRAND (*in utter weariness*):
Oh! to be thousands of miles from ice,
and snow, and naked peaks and rocks!
Oh! how I long for the quiet clocks
that keep the slow time of the South.
There where the Church might be Christ's wife;
and the wine not vinegar in His mouth.
Oh – for the summer kingdoms of life!

BRAND *bursts into tears.*

Jesus! (*Through his tears*) I have cried your name;
but never have your sweet arms come,
to give me rest.
But now, from this prison, my breast,
my heart makes its abject plea,
with Oh! such meaning. Give to me
one fold of your snowy robe to kiss!

GERD (*fearfully*): You are weeping! You!
Warm tears! Why, you will thaw
the glacier, and my Ice Church. Oh!
It's The Thaw! And in my head
something frozen which was dead
moves in my memory – in my breast!
Warm tears! The glacier priest
is slipping off his white surplice and – Oh!
Man, why did you never weep till now?

(*She is trembling*)

BRAND (*looking up radiantly, as if renewed*):
Frost grips the hard phase of The Law;
then comes – like Isaac's ram – The Thaw;

then comes the summer of The Dove,
after the winter of Will! Oh——
The crust is breaking! I can weep. I can kneel.
I can pray! I can pray!

GERD: Watch!

(*Crying out and pointing up*)

Again! The hawk! The hawk! (*She grabs the rifle*)
He brushes the Ice Church with his wings!
If only the bullet will bite——(*She fires the rifle*)

There! That's got him! Look! He falls!

A sound – as of ice creaking and cracking – then a hollow boom like the rolling of thunder follows.

BRAND (*struggling to his feet*):
What have you done? The Ice Church!
It's falling!

Both looking up and off.

GERD: I hit!
He's falling down with the snow.
All his feathers are falling out.
Thousands of white feathers in the air! See!
Look how big and white he grows!

The rumbling, approaching noise grows.

BRAND (*appalled*): The avalanche!
Must we still die
for all the crimes of heredity?   Oh Gerd——

He gathers GERD *close to him as they both look up.*

GERD: *My hawk is dead!*
Look! How he falls, tumbles, rolls,
To the devil with all bad spirits above!
I've no fear now. He's as white as a dove!

As the thundering approach grows she gets afraid.

He's sweeping down over us into the fjord!
He will kill them all!
Oh no! He is going to swallow us up too! Oh!...

GERD *clings to* BRAND, *hiding her head, as he crouches and cries up into the approaching avalanche.*

BRAND : Here! – in this white nothing of death! –
answer me God! – Is there hope above,
for one who with his dying breath
willed *all?*——

The great shadow of the avalanche is closing over them as A VOICE *cries out of the turmoil*

A VOICE: God is Love! . . .

And the statement is echoed from all the rocks, as the sound of the avalanche sweeps on, and down.

FINAL CURTAIN